Alan Titchmarsh
how to garden

Allotment Gardening

BBC
BOOKS

10 9 8 7 6 5 4

Published in 2012 by BBC Books, an imprint of
Ebury Publishing, a Random House Group Company

The Random House Group Limited Reg. No. 954009

Addresses for companies within the Random House
Group can be found at **www.randomhouse.co.uk**

Penguin Random House is committed to a sustainable
future for our business, our readers and our planet.
This book is made from Forest Stewardship council®
certified paper.

A CIP catalogue record for this book is available from
the British Library.

ISBN 978 1 84 990221 2

Produced by OutHouse!
Shalbourne, Marlborough, Wiltshire SN8 3QJ

BBC BOOKS
COMMISSIONING EDITOR: Lorna Russell
PROJECT EDITOR: Caroline McArthur
PRODUCTION: Rebecca Jones

OUTHOUSE!
COMMISSIONING EDITOR: Sue Gordon
SERIES EDITOR & PROJECT EDITOR: Polly Boyd
SERIES ART DIRECTOR: Robin Whitecross
CONTRIBUTING EDITOR: Jo Weeks
DESIGNER: Sharon Cluett
ILLUSTRATIONS by Lizzie Harper, Susan Hillier
PHOTOGRAPHS by Jonathan Buckley except where
credited otherwise on page 96
CONCEPT DEVELOPMENT & SERIES DESIGN:
Elizabeth Mallard-Shaw, Sharon Cluett

Colour origination by Altaimage, London
Printed and bound in China by Leo Paper
Products Ltd.

Contents

Introduction

Gardening is one of the best and most fulfilling activities on earth, but it can sometimes seem complicated and confusing. The answers to problems can usually be found in books, but big fat gardening books can be rather daunting. Where do you start? How can you find just the information you want without wading through lots of stuff that is not appropriate to your particular problem? Well, a good index is helpful, but sometimes a smaller book devoted to one particular subject fits the bill better – especially if it is reasonably priced and if you have a small garden where you might not be able to fit in everything suggested in a larger volume.

The *How to Garden* books aim to fill that gap – even if sometimes it may be only a small one. They are clearly set out and written, I hope, in a straightforward, easy-to-understand style. I don't see any point in making gardening complicated, when much of it is based on common sense and observation. (All the key techniques are explained and illustrated, and I've included plenty of tips and tricks of the trade.)

There are suggestions on the best plants and the best varieties to grow in particular situations and for a particular effect. I've tried to keep the information crisp and to the point so that you can find what you need quickly and easily and then put your new-found knowledge into practice. Don't worry if you're not familiar with the Latin names of plants. They are there to make sure you can find the plant as it will be labelled in the nursery or garden centre, but where appropriate I have included common names, too. Forgetting a plant's name need not stand in your way when it comes to being able to grow it.

Above all, the *How to Garden* books are designed to fill you with passion and enthusiasm for your garden and all that its creation and care entails, from designing and planting it to maintaining it and enjoying it. For more than fifty years gardening has been my passion, and that initial enthusiasm for watching plants grow, for trying something new and for just being outside pottering has never faded. If anything I am keener on gardening now than I ever was and get more satisfaction from my plants every day. It's not that I am simply a romantic, but rather that I have learned to look for the good in gardens and in plants, and there is lots to be found. Oh, there are times when I fail – when my plants don't grow as well as they should and I need to try harder. But where would I rather be on a sunny day? Nowhere!

The *How to Garden* handbooks will, I hope, allow some of that enthusiasm – childish though it may be – to rub off on you, and the information they contain will, I hope, make you a better gardener, as well as opening your eyes to the magic of plants and flowers.

Introducing allotments

There's something very appealing about the idea of setting off to the allotment at the weekend and coming back with a box full of home-grown vegetables and fruit. Allotments attract all sorts of gardeners, but they're particularly important for those who don't have the space in their own back garden to fulfill one of our most basic desires: to provide food for ourselves and our family. There are all sorts of other benefits to growing vegetables in a communal area, including shared plants and growing techniques as well as the informal companionship of like-minded people from all walks of life.

Getting an allotment

Allotments are basically fields divided into little plots, which are then cultivated for food. They are found all around villages, towns and cities, tucked in beside railway lines or beside canals or rivers and other places where pieces of ground have been neglected or left undeveloped for one reason or another. You can rent an allotment for very little money and then, within the rules of the site, it is yours to do what you want with.

Allotments give you a chance to grow a huge range of produce with a view to becoming more self-sufficient.

A brief history of allotments

Although the idea of allotments has been around for centuries, they really took off during the Industrial Revolution, which brought many people from the countryside into the cities. Poorly paid and squeezed into tiny houses, these people often suffered from malnutrition and ill health. The governments of the day tried to address the problem via various acts of Parliament passed to encourage landowners to provide small plots of land for rent so that people could grow their own food for their families. By the early 20th century, allotments were a common feature in cities and towns.

German blockades during the First World War led to food shortages, which then increased the need for home-grown produce, and during the Second World War citizens were encouraged to 'Dig for Victory' by the famous government campaign.

Every spare piece of land was to be put to good use and cultivated for food, including gardens and municipal parks. Allotments had never been so important.

The 1950s and 1960s saw demand for allotments decrease, but in the 1970s there was a surge of interest in self-sufficiency. More recently, fears about chemicals used in food production have resulted in a rise in interest in organic foods and the desire to grow fruit and vegetables. At the beginning of the 21st century, allotments are more popular than ever and demand is huge.

How to get an allotment

In Britain, most allotments are under the control of the local authority, although some are owned and run privately. Contact your local council

The advantages of having an allotment

- Grow your own fresh, organic food.
- Have a much wider range of fruit and veg than is available at supermarkets.
- Very inexpensive pastime and you save money on food.
- Healthy as you get lots of exercise.
- Research shows allotments are relaxing and good for your mental health, too.
- Sociable – you meet people from all walks of life and you can get plenty of free advice.
- Provide a habitat for wildlife and green ecological 'corridors' in urban areas.
- Fun for families – children can learn about gardening and where food comes from and can play outdoors.
- Some allow livestock, such as chickens, rabbits or bees, sometimes for a nominal extra charge.

for information about council-run allotments. They may also be able to tell you about private allotments, but in addition you could get in touch with the National Society of Allotment and Leisure Gardeners (www.nsalg.org.uk) or the Federation of City Farms and Community Gardens (www.farmgarden.org.uk).

If you can't wait …
There is often a long waiting list for allotments. If you're keen to get going, it's well worth popping along to your local allotment site and chatting to some of the current plot-holders. You might find someone who could do with help on their allotment in return for letting you have a portion of the produce. Sharing an allotment is a good way to find out, before you take on a whole plot, whether you're really committed and truly have time to keep one up and running.

It's also worth contacting private individuals who own land and would be prepared to let it in return for some of the produce or a small rent. Landshare (www.landshare.net) is a virtual meeting place that unites people who want somewhere to grow plants with those who have spare ground. Alternatively, you could try putting a sign in a local newsagent's window. It is advisable to sort out financial or practical arrangements before you start to dig.

Location and aspect
If you have a choice of allotment sites, choose one that is within easy reach of your home, preferably walking or cycling distance. The closer the better, as time spent travelling is time that you could be spending enjoying your plot. Also, if it's easy to get to, you're more likely to go more often.

The ideal plot is fairly level or perhaps slopes gently to the south, south east or south west. It should be as sunny as possible. You also want a site with some protection from the prevailing wind, which usually comes from the south west, as well as cold winds from the north and north east. Although a gentle breeze moving over your plot is a good thing, because it will bring in pollinating insects and deter pests and some diseases, too much wind can have a devastating effect on crops and will shorten your growing season. If there is no existing protection and the allotment is in an exposed site, factor in windbreaks or low fences when planning your plot (*see* page 37).

Brussels sprouts are a great allotment crop – they're almost foolproof, provide healthy food through the winter and taste so much better than if you buy them.

Rent and tenancy agreements

You do have to pay rent for an allotment. However, rents are extremely good value. The average annual cost is £40–60 for an average full-sized plot (*see* page 11), with reductions for pensioners and those on low incomes; in London, prices are higher and may be as much as £100. A smaller plot will be cheaper.

Usually, you will have to sign a tenancy agreement, which will set down how much your rent will be, when you have to pay it and rules that apply on site, such as siting and size of sheds and other structures and whether or not you can keep livestock. The rules and conditions vary greatly across the country and from one allotment site to another.

Most agreements last for one year and can be renewed indefinitely. If you decide to give up within a year, there are usually plenty of people willing to take your place. Allotment supervisors are unlikely to hold you to a year's contract, so long as you leave your plot in reasonably good order.

This neatly laid out, flat and sunny plot has everything, including a lovely view beyond a dense shelterbelt of trees.

Ideally, choose a plot that is tucked away in the middle, where you will be sheltered by the other plots and there are less likely to be large trees or high fencing casting heavy shade. Being away from the perimeter also means you may be safer from vandalism, which can be a problem in some areas (less so if the site is surrounded by a strong fence or thick, thorny hedge). In addition, you're less likely to be plagued by rabbits and squirrels, which may sneak in from surrounding fields, hedgerows or wasteland to feed on your allotment vegetables and fruit.

Size and shape

The plots you get on most allotment sites tend to be rectangular. They vary greatly, but about 10 'rods' or 'poles' (the length of an ox and a plough), or 252 square metres (300 square yards), is about average for a full-size plot. This is the space deemed by various acts of Parliament as being enough to 'feed a family of four', and it will certainly seem very big if you're new to growing your own. It is often better to opt for a smaller area to start with until you gain confidence and experience. Some allotment sites offer half- or even quarter-sized plots.

Once you get the hang of growing fruit and vegetables, you might find you want to take on some more land. Depending on how popular your allotment site is, this can be an option, although you may have to wait some time before it comes free.

Soil

A major factor in whether your vegetable-growing is going to be a success is the soil, so it's worth

Don't forget

Some allotments have trading sheds where you can buy equipment, seeds and fertilizers. These can come in very handy when you have only a limited amount of time to spare and can't get to the shops.

assessing this early on. If the soil is easily visible when you inherit the allotment you're in luck, as it means the previous occupant has obviously cultivated it fairly recently. Dense, healthy weeds mean it is likely to be fairly rich in nutrients – nettles in particular indicate fertile soil. In summer, lush weed growth shows there is plenty of moisture available in the soil, too.

Use a fork or spade to turn the soil over and examine its condition. Dark, easily dug soil containing lots of worms is a sign of a well-tended plot. Dig in a few places, as you may find different conditions over even a relatively small area. Some parts may be very damp, indicating poor drainage, while others might be extremely dry. You may find stones or old rubbish – places where it will be difficult to grow plants.

The condition, texture and acidity of your soil (see page 20) will have a bearing on what produce you can grow in your allotment and whether or not you decide to build raised beds (see pages 14, 15 and 23).

> ### Don't forget
> Adding well-rotted compost and other humus-rich material to any soil type will improve growing conditions for the plants (see pages 24–5).

Water is a priority. Here, each shed has guttering and a large butt to ensure a generous supply.

Water

Water is vital for healthy fruit and vegetables, so you need to think how you are going to get it onto your plot. Most allotments have taps available for use by the tenants, although there may be regulations about how often you can use them and whether you can use hosepipes or are restricted to watering cans. The allotment site manager should let you know about any rules, but if not, ask before you make free with the water supply.

Have a look to see what other tenants are doing about water, too. This will give you a few ideas. They will probably be making use of a range of water-saving methods, particularly water butts. This is where sheds or greenhouses come in useful, since you can put guttering around them and collect any rainfall.

There's nothing like a patch of healthy, well-dug and weed-free soil to make you want to get sowing and planting.

Planning your plot

When you're full of enthusiasm and faced with a plotful of weeds, it's tempting to get stuck in and start digging, but you'll find everything goes more smoothly if you think carefully about the layout of the allotment you've inherited and reassess it if necessary. Think about what produce you'll want to grow and how, and consider whether you can make any improvements.

Deciding what to grow

You may already have a good idea of what you want to grow in your allotment, but it helps to make a list, partly to ensure you don't forget anything and partly to act as a reality check on some of your more ambitious plans. Remember to include fruit as well as vegetables, and winter crops along with summer salads. Don't feel that you ought to grow food that you don't particularly like, but remember that home-grown produce always tastes better, so it pays to keep an open mind. Remember, too, that you'll need to store a certain amount of produce, such as potatoes and onions, so make sure you have a suitable place to keep them. Some fruit and vegetables freeze better than others, and this may also determine what you decide to grow (*see* page 43).

Your list will probably be very long, so prioritize it. It is sensible to start with just a few of your favourites and extend the list as you gain experience and confidence. You'll also find it very useful to chat

A well-planned allotment includes shelter for young plants, protection for fruit and a variety of supports for climbers.

What's easy to grow and what's not

EASY		MORE DEMANDING	
Apples*	Kale	Aubergines	Peas
Artichokes, globe	Leeks	Beetroot	Plums
Artichokes, Jerusalem	Onions, shallots	Blueberries	Radishes
Asparagus	Peppers	Broad beans	Spinach
Blackberries*	Perpetual spinach	Cabbages	Sweetcorn
Broccoli (sprouting)	Potatoes	Carrots	Tomatoes (cordon)
Brussels sprouts	Pumpkins, squashes	Celeriac	
Chicory	Raspberries*	Chicory (for forcing)	MOST DEMANDING
Chillies	Rhubarb	Cucumbers	Calabrese
Courgettes, marrows	Runner beans	Endive	Cauliflowers
Currants*	Salad leaves	French beans	Celery
Garlic	Strawberries	Kiwis	Florence fennel
Gooseberries*	Swedes	Kohl rabi	Grapes
Herbs	Swiss chard	Lettuces	Pears
	Tomatoes (bush)	Parsnips	
	Turnips		* Easy but need pruning

to fellow allotment-holders to find out what is likely to grow well at your site and what could possibly struggle. They'll be able to give you vital information about the soil type (*see* page 20) as well as the usual weather conditions, including when to expect the first and last frosts.

Planning beds

Ideally, you will have at least four main beds. One will be permanent, to include perennial crops such as asparagus, globe artichokes, soft fruit and rhubarb. All except rhubarb need a sunny site.

In addition, designate at least three other beds for all the other vegetables. This will enable you to carry out a three-year crop rotation scheme (*see* page 27). You can have more beds if you like, in which case you could work a four- or even five-year rotation. You should also

Don't forget

Unless the previous occupant of your allotment has left it in very good order, to begin with you will have to dig, even if you are having raised beds (see opposite and page 23).

include a seed bed or nursery bed (*see* pages 28–9) and you may like a bed for ornamentals, where you can grow flowers for cutting.

Ground-level or raised beds?

You can create beds at ground level or make raised beds (*see* opposite and page 23). Many people prefer raised beds, because once they're constructed you can get growing more quickly, you don't need to dig as they don't become compacted, and they create ideal conditions for growing vegetables, particularly if your allotment soil is very stony, heavy or light (*see* page 20). However, provided your soil is good and you don't mind a bit more digging at the preparation stage, ground-level beds should be fine (and are less costly).

A good compromise is to have a mixture of ground-level and raised beds – ground-level beds for those vegetables that will thrive in the soil in your allotment, and raised beds for those that need to grow in certain conditions, such as carrots and parsnips, which do best in stone-free, light, well-drained soil.

Shape and size

Beds can, in theory, be any shape you like. Bear in mind, though, that rectangular beds are traditional for a good reason. They make the most of the space available and allow you to grow neat rows of vegetables. Also, you can work between such rows very easily – watering, hoeing and so on. If you decide to go for triangles or other unusual shapes, you may end up with odd corners that are difficult to fill.

The width of the beds depends on what you plan to cultivate and how. As far as possible, you want to avoid treading on the soil; you need to be able to reach the middle of the bed from the path. Ground-level beds are ideally between 1m (3ft) and 1.2m (4ft) wide. Raised beds often need to be narrower (*see* page 23).

Beds containing permanent plants are usually best on the perimeter of the plot, where they can cast shade over boundary paths, rather than on your crops. It might be an idea to make these a little bigger than the rest, since the plants in them could grow rather large.

Dividing large beds

Within each large bed you should create several subdivisions, with paths between for access. A major advantage of doing this is that it clearly breaks down your work into smaller, more manageable chunks – you can tend a small, self-contained area at each visit, for example.

Dividing a plot into neat, well-defined rectangular beds, easily accessed by paths, helps to make it easy to maintain.

Raised beds

Raised beds are basically frames into which soil and plenty of organic matter are piled. They can be as low as one plank of wood (say 15cm/6in), up to any sensible height, although about 40cm (16in) is a reasonable maximum on an allotment: you have to fill them after all.

Advantages and disadvantages

Raised beds are ideal if you have a very stony, heavy or light soil. Because raised beds sit above the ground, they tend to be free-draining, comparatively weed-free and easy to weed when necessary. They are never walked on, so the soil doesn't become compacted, which means they rarely need digging, and because of the organic matter and the loose soil, plants find it easier to grow in them. This means you should be able to get more crops in less space. Sitting above ground means that the soil in them warms up earlier in spring, which is another big advantage.

Raised beds are great if you don't have lots of time for digging, or have limitations on how much you can dig. Because they divide your plot up into smaller portions, they make it much more manageable. They also look neat and can be made in all sorts of shapes and sizes, so could even transform a boring plot into a beautifully designed potager, if that's what you want.

There are a few downsides to raised beds. For a start, you need to buy or make them (*see* page 23), which can often be costly. Then you'll need to source some good-quality topsoil and lots of organic matter. Raised beds also need quite a bit more watering than ground-level ones.

Raised beds are a great way to grow vegetables.

① Each bed can be devoted to a different group of vegetables.

② Tomatoes do well in the warm, fertile, well-drained soil.

③ The easy growing conditions ensure long, straight, tender carrots.

Do I need raised beds?

As you assessed your plot (*see* pages 11–12 and 20) you will have noticed various things about the soil. If you can answer yes to the following questions, you really ought to use raised beds, even if you quite like digging.

■ Was the soil stony and hard to dig? It is rarely worth trying to clear stones from the soil. A few large stones can be put to one side, but lots in various sizes will keep you busy forever. Plants can grow around stones, but they make it difficult for seeds to germinate and roots to grow, as well as making the general growing conditions poor and drainage uneven.

■ Was the soil claggy and wet? Very heavy soil that is poorly drained is not good for plants, as roots find it hard to penetrate and it takes a long time to warm up in spring. You will need to add plenty of humus-rich material over several years before you start seeing a definite improvement.

■ Is the subsoil near the surface? Subsoil is usually a different colour (often paler) from the topsoil. A shallow layer of topsoil presents difficulties for plants because subsoil has a poor structure and low fertility. Again, it takes a lot of work and many years to improve its condition.

Practical paths

Paths are essential on the allotment, to ensure that you avoid walking on cultivated ground and compacting the soil. You'll need to include boundary paths (around the plot) and main paths (between the beds) as well as narrow access paths that will divide up large beds to make maintenance easier – for example, when watering, weeding, harvesting and pruning.

The ideal width for main paths is at least 60cm (2ft) – wide enough to accommodate a wheelbarrow – but you can make access paths narrower, as long as you accept that you'll be tramping up and down to the wheelbarrow stranded on the wider path. Make sure that you have an easy route between the beds, the compost heap and the water supply.

Don't forget

Low-growing plants, such as stepover apples or herbs, make good path edgings (see page 31).

Surfacing options

It is well worth surfacing allotment paths in some way, because they will get slippery and muddy when wet. Surfacing also has the effect of making the whole plot look tidy and well cared for.

The quickest surface is bark chippings. These can be laid directly on the weed-free soil. Walk up and down a few times to compact it first. With raised beds, the sides of the bed will keep the chippings in place. Bark will rot down after a couple of years, but you can either put more on top or shovel the old stuff onto the compost heap and start again.

Other options include paving stones, which you might get fairly cheaply second hand, or hardcore (this works better than gravel, which can get stuck to muddy boots). Rolls of plastic material made especially for paths look good and are quick to lay, but the downside is that they're comparatively costly.

Grass paths are very traditional on allotments. However, if you're regularly using them the grass may suffer and it will tend to become muddy in wet weather and migrate into surrounding beds if they're not raised. Other drawbacks are that you'll need to mow the grass and store a mower or strimmer.

Sheds and other permanent features

It's worth making a note of what other allotment-holders have got on their sites, since this will give you some ideas about the permanent features you might like to include.

Make do and mend

Before splashing out on brand new sheds, water butts and so on, bear in mind that allotments are quite different from gardens – they aren't near your house and they don't need to be highly ornamental. Think about reusing any household items and scrap that you find on skips or at car-boot sales, and look in your local paper or newsagent's window for bargains.

You can either use the items as they are – perhaps you have an old chair or bench you don't want any more – or, with a little ingenuity, you can adapt them to make something else. For instance, you can construct a makeshift cold frame from window panes and bricks, or a compost bin out of discarded pallets and bits of timber. On a smaller scale, empty plastic water bottles with the base cut off make ideal cloches for seedlings, and you can make an effective bird scarer by hanging unwanted CDs and DVDs along a length of string (see page 23; the birds mistake the discs for the eyes of a predator). As well as being highly practical, these improvised items will help to make your allotment feel more of a personal space.

Paths are easy to make and invaluable for getting around the plot. Chipped bark is an inexpensive, practical surface.

Finding ways to personalize your plot, such as this shed, is fun and a great way to develop your creative side.

Check your allotment regulations to see if there are any restrictions on where you can place sheds and other structures. If not, sheds, water butts and compost bins can go in a shady or damp spot if you have one, while cold frames and greenhouses need plenty of sunshine. Avoid placing a greenhouse at the bottom of a slope, because cold air sinks and this is likely to be a much cooler spot than elsewhere on your allotment. Position your shed in a convenient situation where it won't cast too much shade. You might even be able to place it where it can reduce the speed of the wind over your plot.

Get the largest shed and greenhouse that you can afford, because the space is always useful. Make sure they will fit comfortably on your plot, of course, and are allowed by your site's regulations.

Sheds, greenhouses and water butts all need a firm foundation. Square fencing posts do a good job; alternatively, you could use paving slabs. If you can, raise wooden sheds off the ground on bricks to prevent the wood from rotting. If you're on a slope, you may need to dig out an area to create a level site.

Rest and recreation areas

Make life more enjoyable and comfortable for yourself and your family on the allotment – it's not just about hard work. You might want to have a play area for the kids to entertain themselves while you are

digging (position this away from potential hazards, such as cold frames). It's also a very good idea to include a seating area for when you want to relax at the end of a hard day's digging, or when you've just popped in to pick up some veg or fruit on your way home from the office. Keep a small gas stove, a few mugs, tea bags, a bottle of water and matches in an airtight tin in the shed so you can have a restorative cuppa.

You can create a 'cutting garden' for sweet peas, or grow them with your vegetables. They'll love the rich soil.

Allotment checklist

When planning your allotment, use the checklist below to ensure you haven't left out anything important, although you may not need all of the elements.

■ Permanent bed (one or more for herbs, artichokes, asparagus and fruit)
■ Crop-rotation beds (three beds minimum, see page 27)
■ Nursery bed or seed bed (one or more, see pages 28–9)
■ Cutting garden
■ Paths – boundary, main and access (see opposite)
■ Stepover apples along paths (see page 31)
■ Seating area
■ Play area

■ Shed and/or other storage
■ Compost bins x 3 (see page 25)
■ Manure storage
■ Water butts (one or more near shed to collect rainwater)
■ Cold frames (see page 38)
■ Tunnel cloches (plastic, netting, horticultural fleece) (see pages 37–8)
■ Bell/lantern cloches (glass, plastic, bamboo)
■ Greenhouse/polytunnel (see page 38)
■ Fruit cage (see page 38)
■ Bird scarers
■ Windbreaks (see page 37)
■ Drainage trench (for wet sites)

Planting and growing

When you have an allotment, you'll want to achieve maximum yields from your crops: if you're going to spend your precious time working on the plot, it needs to repay you. As most longstanding vegetable gardeners will tell you, there's no substitute for hard work, but the physical energy put in can be very enjoyable as well as rewarding. With gardening, as with most things, the best way to avoid wasting energy is to do it right first time, and this is where the following pages should be able to help.

Tools and equipment

You'll need a range of gardening tools to be able to work on your allotment. There are a few that you'll want to get straight away, while others can be added over time. Don't feel you have to rush out and buy a whole variety of equipment before you know exactly what you're going to use it for. Wait until you find you need something, then buy the best you can afford.

Keep your shed tidy by having a hook for each tool.

Fork Essential for breaking up areas of compacted soil and extricating stones and troublesome weeds.

Spade An indispensable tool for digging, shovelling compost and other organic material onto beds and making planting holes.

Mattock Comes in handy for heavy digging. It consists of a wide blade opposite a narrow one, set at right angles to a thick shaft. You use it in a chopping motion, like a pick.

Hoe There are several types of hoe available. A Dutch (or 'push') hoe is used by sliding the blade just under the soil surface and it slices weeds as it goes; it also loosens the surface of the soil. A draw (or 'chop') hoe is used in a chopping motion to cut down weeds. It is also useful for making seed drills and earthing up plants. For more delicate work, such as weeding around seedlings, onions and strawberries, or in raised beds, use an onion hoe – a short-handled, light version of the draw hoe.

Parallel-toothed rake Needed for preparing seed beds and breaking up the surface of newly dug soil.

Trowel and hand fork Essential for planting, weeding and lifting small plants.

Secateurs, loppers and saw Needed for pruning stems and branches, depending on their thickness (*see* page 39).

Canes Invaluable bamboo poles of differing thicknesses and lengths for supporting plants, including beans and peas, and holding netting.

Protective coverings Cloches, cold frames and horticultural fleece protect against cold, wind and birds.

Plastic netting Plastic netting is ideal for keeping birds off crops and for supporting taller plants.

Rabbit-proof fencing Heavy-duty chicken wire, 1m (3ft) high, buried a spade's depth in the ground, keeps rabbits off your crops.

Seed trays, cell trays, pots If raising plants from seed indoors, you'll need trays or pots for sowing and growing on seedlings.

Dibber A pointed tool used for making holes when sowing seed. You can make one out of broken tool handles or a pencil.

Containers for water You'll need at least one water butt to collect rainwater; it could just be an old bath. You'll also need at least one watering can. A hosepipe with spray attachment is useful, too.

Bucket and trug For carrying compost and harvested produce.

Wheelbarrow For transporting soil and manure around the plot.

Pegs and string Needed for marking out lines of vegetables.

Plant labels and a marker pen For labelling different crops.

Garden knife and soft twine For general maintenance jobs such as tying back plants.

Gardening gloves Available in different thicknesses for various jobs.

Notebook and pen It's a good idea to record what you planted in each bed each year.

All about soil

Knowing something about your soil will help you to grow better crops. Depending on where you live, soil is made up of differing amounts of clay, sand, loam, chalk (limestone) and peat. If it isn't much good for growing vegetables, take heart – there are lots of ways to improve the soil (*see* pages 24–6), and you can always make raised beds filled with the ideal growing medium.

Soil texture

Most crops grow well in loam. It is easy to dig, fertile and moisture-retentive while also draining well.

Sandy soil warms up quickly in spring, so is good for early crops. It is light, which allows root crops, such as carrots, to grow well in it. It is also free-draining, which can make it dry and means nutrients can be washed away quickly. Dig in well-rotted farmyard manure, to improve water retention and add nutrients, and liquid feed regularly.

Clay soil is moisture-retentive and rich in nutrients, but its dense texture is hard for roots to penetrate and it is slow to warm up in spring. Most crops grow well in clay, as long as the drainage is improved with lots of organic matter: good preparation work is particularly important if you have a clay soil.

Chalky soil is often stony and the topsoil is quite shallow, so if you have this type of soil raised beds are often the best option. It is free-draining and warms up quickly in spring. It is usually alkaline (*see* below), making it good for growing brassicas.

Peaty soil is lightweight and moisture-retentive. However, it is very low in nutrients, which means that it needs plenty of fertilizer and manure to increase its fertility. It is usually found in high rainfall areas and can be poorly drained, making raised beds a good choice.

Soil pH

pH is a measurement of the acid–alkaline balance in soil. Very acid is pH1, pH7 is neutral and pH14 is very alkaline. Most vegetables seem to grow best on soil that is neutral, but brassicas require alkaline soil. Most fruit prefers neutral to slightly acid soil. You can find out the acidity or alkalinity of your soil by buying an inexpensive soil-testing kit from any garden centre. If your soil is acid, you can add lime to it to slightly increase its alkalinity for your brassicas (*see* page 25).

Identifying your soil type

Before you decide which vegetables and fruit to grow on your allotment, your first step should be to find out what type of soil you have, as it has an impact on how well different plants grow. The five main types are illustrated here, but your particular soil might not be clearly one or another. It's possible to have a mixture of soils, say peaty loam or chalky clay.

① Sandy soil feels gritty, like sand at the beach. Take a handful and it will feel light and pour out between your fingers rather than forming a ball, because it's loose-textured and usually dry.

② Clay soil feels heavy and sticky, and can be rolled into a smooth ball. It forms lumps when wet, and is hard and solid when dry.

③ Chalky soil is usually full of pale lumps of chalk, which crumble if you rub them together. The soil has a loose texture, making it easy to dig.

④ Loam is even-textured, feels soft and is a mid- to dark brown. It can be squeezed into a ball, but if it is rubbed it easily breaks into crumbs again.

⑤ Peat is very dark and open-textured, almost like a sponge. It holds on to water well, but can be rather crumbly and difficult to rewet when it does dry out.

Don't forget

The effect of adding lime is only short-lived, so you need to test your soil annually and add it most years if necessary.

Preparing the ground for planting

The optimum time to take over a plot is in autumn or early winter. This is because the main growing season is spring to autumn, so you'll have a few months in which to prepare the soil. If you start off in spring or early summer, you'll need to work hard but can still grow a wide range of produce; a late-summer start may mean restricting yourself to overwintering vegetables.

Removing weeds

Depending on the condition of your allotment when you take it on, you'll probably have to start by removing weeds. A very overgrown plot may be a bit daunting at first, but you'll be amazed at how different it will look after a couple of hours' work.

Begin by using secateurs and, if necessary, pruning loppers, to clear as much of the top-growth as you can. Wear thick gloves to protect your hands. If the site is very over-grown, look into hiring a brushcutter for a weekend to do the really tough work. You may find perennial fruit and vegetable plants, for example rhubarb or blackcurrants, among the weeds, so be careful as you hack.

Once you've got things down to a reasonable height, you have two options. The first and easiest is to use weedkiller to get rid of all the plants you don't want; the second

and much more labour-intensive option is to dig them out by hand, or you can use a rotavator. Some allotment organizations will run a rotavator over your plot before you take it over, and this can be helpful, but rotavators do have a drawback: if there are any perennial weed roots in the soil, the machine's blades will cut them up, effectively propagating the weeds, since they can grow from even the tiniest pieces of root. The advantage of rotavating is that the soil should be loose enough for you to be able to pull up any new weed growth. Make sure you do this as soon as the growth appears.

Using weedkillers

Most people are a bit wary about using weedkiller, but the only variety that is widely available is based on glyphosate, which becomes inactive once it hits the soil. This means that its effect on the environment is believed to be minimal. Even determinedly organic growers will often clear a plot with glyphosate and avoid chemicals from then on.

Don't forget

Try to remove as much of any perennial weed roots as you can, because most of these can regrow from even the tiniest piece. Never compost the fresh roots unless you kill them off first (see Don't Forget, page 24).

Some digging is almost inevitable when you take over a plot, but it is a good way to get to know your soil.

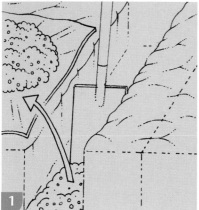

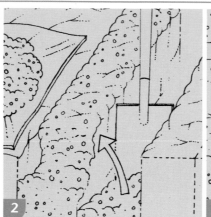

1 Dig trenches across the width of the bed. Make the first trench about a spit (spade's blade) deep and the same across. Set aside the soil you've dug, putting it onto a piece of plastic sheeting or in a wheelbarrow. Fork over the base of the trench and then pile in plenty of compost.

2 Dig a second trench beside the first, and transfer the soil from the second trench into the first one. Don't worry about doing it neatly. The most important things are to dig fairly deep, break up dense clumps of soil and add lots of compost. Continue in this way until you get to the final trench.

3 When you've dug the last trench at the far end of the bed, pile plenty of compost into it. Then fill the trench with the soil on the sheeting or in the wheelbarrow that was taken from the first trench. Go over the whole area and break up any lumps with a fork.

Weedkillers are not an immediate cure-all, however. You'll need to apply them according to the manufacturer's instructions, then wait for them to do their work. Once the weeds die down, you'll have to dig them out, then it is sensible to wait again for any regrowth. Treat this with another dose of weedkiller before you start any planting.

Weeding by hand
If you decide to remove weeds by hand, begin at one end of the bed and work your way to the other, using a fork to dig out weeds, particularly perennial weed roots. A mattock can come in useful for heavy digging. If the weather is dry and the soil fairly light, digging out weeds is satisfying work and has the benefit of working over the plot too, which makes the rest of your preparation a bit easier.

Suppressing weed growth
As soon as you've cleared a bed of weeds, if you're not going to sow or plant straight away you need to cover the ground to prevent any weed seeds from germinating. Black plastic or weedproof membrane is often used, but thick cardboard (as used in the packaging of electronic and white goods) is even better, as it is environmentally friendly and cost-free. Simply lay the covering over the bare ground, hold down the edges with stones, bricks or water-filled plastic bottles and leave

Don't forget
Potatoes and Jerusalem artichokes are good vegetables to grow when you're bringing an area into cultivation for the first time or after long neglect; the way they're grown and their leafy foliage help to suppress weed growth.

it in place until you need to sow or plant. If you're using cardboard, it will rot down naturally over time and will be taken down by the worms, adding to the soil's fertility.

Another good way of suppressing weeds in bare soil is to sow a green manure (see box, page 26).

Digging over the plot
If you're not going to have raised beds, and if your soil hasn't been cultivated for a while, single digging is probably the best way to prepare your plot for planting. When you single dig, you excavate a trench to the depth of a spade blade and add composted material (see above).

Once you've done this initial deep dig, unless there is a disaster, such as a flood, or bad compaction occurs for some reason, there is no real need to do it again. It is enough to add compost or other humus-rich material on a regular basis, either piling it as a mulch on the soil surface or gently incorporating it into the top few inches using a fork. You may also like to add slow-release fertilizers (*see* page 26).

Constructing raised beds

If the soil on your allotment plot is not very good quality – perhaps it's heavy and difficult to dig, shallow, poorly drained or very stony – you'll probably want to make raised beds (*see also* pages 14 and 15).

Once you've decided on the site of your raised beds, you'll need to dig the ground over thoroughly to get rid of weeds, remove any large stones and use a fork to loosen areas of compacted soil to assist drainage.

Height and size

Even creating a raised bed only a few centimetres above the ground will have an impact on your growing conditions. You can buy raised beds from garden centres and DIY shops, or you can make them yourself (*see* right). Around 15–20cm (6–8in) is a good minimum height for most allotment beds. Consider increasing the height to 30–40cm (12–16in) on very poorly drained soil, heavy clay, and for nursery beds and plants that need particular conditions, such as carrots or herbs.

The maximum width of a raised bed that you can access from both

sides is 1.2–1.5m (4–5ft), so you can reach the middle without stretching. Halve this if you can work only from one side. Raised beds can be any length, but if they're very long you may be tempted to walk across them to avoid the trek to the other side.

Making and filling the beds

There are many ways to construct a raised bed, but on an allotment, where the look isn't a priority, you'll probably want to keep things as simple as possible.

To make a basic bed 90cm (3ft) wide and 15cm (6in) high, you will need four 15cm- (6in-) wide wooden planks (two at 1.2m/4ft long, two at 90cm/3ft long) and four wooden posts, 50 x 50mm (2 x 2in) thick and 45cm (18in) long. Always use wood that has been treated for outdoor use. Select planks of a decent

thickness, about 35–40mm (1½–1¾in), because they have to hold a considerable weight of soil – scaffolding planks are ideal as they are very sturdy.

To make a higher bed, use two planks of wood, one on top of the other, or wider planks, and increase the length of the posts – always allow for a reasonable depth to go into the ground, 30cm (12in) is ideal. For a longer bed, you may need to use more supporting posts to give added strength, depending on the length of the bed and the thickness of the planks.

Once you've made the raised bed, fork over the base once more to ensure the soil isn't compacted, then fill the bed with a mixture of good-quality topsoil and well-rotted compost or farmyard manure. Half and half is ideal for vegetables.

These raised beds are easy to access on all sides. The long corner posts can be used for supporting bird scarers, netting and other protection.

Adding soil improvers

To grow fruit and vegetables well you need healthy, fertile soil, and you can achieve this by using lots of well-rotted organic material along with some slow-release fertilizers. Organic matter is traditionally added in the autumn, so it has time to mix with the soil before spring planting begins, while slow-release fertilizers are used between late winter and early spring, so they are available to the plants throughout the growing season.

Adding organic matter

After clearing the site, and once a year thereafter, it's important to add humus-rich organic matter, such as well-rotted manure or garden compost, to most beds; those that are going to contain root vegetables next season are an exception (*see* Crop rotation, page 27).

Organic matter will improve drainage, hold on to moisture and increase the amount of air contained in the soil – all of which are good for plants. It also contains numerous beneficial organisms that continue to break it down into ever-smaller particles, gradually releasing nutrients back into the soil.

Ideally, add organic matter in autumn; you can spread it thickly over the surface, and worms and other organisms will work it into the soil before the main growing season. In spring or summer, they won't have had time, so it's best to dig it in.

Making compost

Garden compost is one of the major sources of good organic material and is one of the keys to success in fruit- and vegetable-growing. It is almost impossible to use too much

Old mushroom compost can be used to improve soil texture, but it contains few nutrients.

of it, and the great thing about it is that it costs nothing. It is also very easy to make: when you have your allotment up and running, you'll be adding to the compost heap almost continuously, recycling plant material and other household waste without much effort at all.

There are a few simple rules for making good compost. You can use most organic material, with some exceptions (*see* box, opposite). To ensure even rotting, you need to combine dry materials, such as plant stalks, with moist ones, for example bolted lettuce. Also, mix thicker materials with finer ones, since this will reduce the need for turning the heap, which is a lot of work. Cut up

Don't forget

Although you can't use fresh perennial weed roots on the compost heap, you can kill them off first and then use them. Either soak them in water for about three weeks, then put them on the compost heap, or insert them in plastic bags, leave them for a year and add the resulting slime to the compost heap or dig it straight into the ground.

The composting area is one of the most important and useful places on the allotment. Try to have several bins, and make sure that they're easy to access.

large stalks and woody material so that they rot more quickly. If you have lots of nettles, cut these up, discard the roots, and mix the leaves and stems with your compost, since they speed up decomposition.

Check your compost regularly and water it if it seems dry or isn't rotting down. You can cover it to keep the moisture in and the temperature up. Old carpet (hessian-backed wool, not foam-backed synthetic fibre) is ideal if it is allowed on your allotment site, but you can also cover the heap in black plastic sheeting.

Compost bins

If you have the space, it's best to have three compost bins on the allotment: one to contain the stuff that is rotting down, one for your current waste and one that contains the ready compost. Two will do, so long as you can empty the ready compost onto the plot. Wooden bins of about one cubic metre (cubic yard) are a good size. They are easy to make, or there are many designs for sale, including plastic 'dustbin' type ones, which are smaller.

Most fruit and vegetables grow considerably better when plenty of compost has been added to their beds in spring or autumn.

Adding lime

You'll probably hear your fellow allotment-holders talking about liming the soil. It sounds rather technical, but the theory is quite simple. Most vegetables grow best on neutral soil. Adding farmyard manure and compost to the soil gradually increases its acidity, so lime, which is alkaline, may need to be added to reduce it. (For more on soil pH, see page 20.)

Lime is sold either as gardener's lime, calcified seaweed or ground chalk. All are fine powders that are sprinkled over the soil in the autumn, so that they can be washed in over the winter. Add lime about three or four weeks before you add your compost. The overall effect is only slight, however, and rain will wash it out of the soil, so liming is only a temporary measure.

Brassicas

Cauliflowers, cabbages, broccoli and other members of the cabbage family are called brassicas, and they much prefer to grow on slightly alkaline soil. This also reduces the risk of clubroot, so depending on your soil pH, you may need to add lime to their bed annually.

Compost ingredients	
DO INCLUDE	DO NOT INCLUDE
Grass clippings	Cooked food
Leaves (including weed leaves)	Roots of perennial weeds (e.g. dandelion, bindweed, couch grass), unless treated (see Don't Forget, opposite)
Annual weeds that haven't seeded	
Vegetable peelings	
Tea bags and coffee grounds	Seedheads of annual weeds
Crushed eggshells	Thick branches and thorny stems, e.g. brambles
Paper tissues	
Cotton wool	Diseased plants
Old newspapers and cardboard (shredded)	Coal ashes
Hair	Glossy magazines
Droppings from guinea pigs or rabbits	Cat and dog muck
Chicken manure	

Plant foods

Plant foods, or fertilizers, are used to provide plants with the nutrients they need for healthy growth and crop production. There are two types – slow-release fertilizers that are added during soil preparation, which are described here, and those that you apply as regular feeds during the growing season, which are covered on page 35.

Slow-release fertilizers come as pellets, granules and powders. They are added to the soil in late winter or early spring, just before you start planting. You can scatter them over the surface or lightly dig them into the soil. As their name suggests, they will gradually release their nutrients into the soil and will be available to the plants throughout the growing season.

Generally, plants need three key nutrients: nitrogen (N), for leaf production; phosphate (P), for roots; and potassium (K), or potash, for flowers and fruit. They also require minute quantities of a variety of micronutrients. All fertilizers contain these in varying amounts.

There are two main types of slow-release fertilizer: chemical (or inorganic) and organic. There are pros and cons for each.

Chemical fertilizers These contain measured amounts of the three principle nutrients in equal quantities. They are most likely to provide your plants with what they require, but do nothing for the long-term health of the soil or its micro-organisms, and there are concerns about the effect they are having on the environment. Growmore is the most well known of the inorganic fertilizers.

Organic feeds These are usually made from natural ingredients or animal by-products; the most familiar ones are seaweed, poultry manure, bonemeal and blood, fish and bone. Organic feeds may contain plenty of the three chief nutrients, but the amounts are not equal, so they are less 'balanced' than chemical feeds. Organic feeds should generally be more environmentally friendly, but you do need to consider their origin: for example, whether the poultry manure pellets are from free-range or factory-farmed chickens.

Slow-release fertilizers can be sprinkled around the base of plants to give them a long-lasting source of food.

Don't forget

Recommended quantities vary depending on the type of fertilizer, so always follow the instructions on the back of the packet.

Green manures

Another way of increasing soil fertility and suppressing weed growth is to sow green manures. These are fast-growing crops that are raised on empty beds and then dug back into the soil, stems and all, at least four weeks before crop-planting. They include clover and alfalfa, and they add nitrogen to the soil, as well as improving its structure and increasing the general humus content when dug back in. Green manures can be sown in late summer, for digging back in autumn, or in autumn, for overwintering.

The idea behind crop rotation (moving groups of plants to different beds each year) is to avoid planting the same crop in the same ground year after year, thus giving your plants the best chance of doing well. Although it doesn't guarantee success, it certainly makes a lot of sense, particularly for growers who want to avoid using chemicals.

Most vegetables belong to one of three main groups:
① Legumes
② Brassicas
③ Root vegetables

What are the benefits?

There are two main reasons for crop rotation. First, it is a natural way of controlling pests and diseases. If you were to grow the same crop in the same piece of ground again and again, certain pests and diseases that affect that particular crop would inevitably build up, particularly in the soil. However, by moving plants to different beds each year you avoid the health problems getting out of control, or even occurring in the first place.

Another benefit of crop rotation is to ensure that each type of crop gets what it needs in the way of nutrients. Each different crop has its own specific requirements, and if you grow the same crop in the same place over consecutive years these nutrients will eventually be in short supply, because the plants will have drained the soil in previous years. By moving the crops and adding the appropriate soil improver to each bed, you will ensure all your vegetables get the conditions that they like best to enable them to thrive.

How to rotate crops

The technique of crop rotation is straightforward: vegetables are divided into groups according to their ideal growing conditions and each year these groups are grown in a different bed. Traditionally, plots were divided into four or even five main areas (with potatoes or onions in a bed on their own), but a three-year, three-bed rotation is sufficient for most gardeners.

The three-year plan shown on the left revolves around three main vegetable groups: the legumes (peas and beans), the brassicas and the root vegetables. The roots of the legumes are packed with nitrogen and will help enrich the soil when they break down. For this reason, they are usually followed by brassicas, which like plenty of nitrogen. The root vegetables don't require much nitrogen (in fact too much can cause 'fanging' in carrots and parsnips), so they usually follow the brassicas.

Three-year crop-rotation scheme

Below is a chart showing a suggested three-year crop-rotation scheme. Any vegetables not on the chart (except globe artichokes and asparagus, which need permanent beds) can be slotted into empty spaces in any of the beds. The main thing is that none of the vegetables listed should be grown in the same place two years running.

	BED 1	BED 2	BED 3
YEAR 1	**Legumes** Beans Peas	**Brassicas** Broccoli Brussels sprouts Cabbages Calabrese Cauliflowers Kale Kohl rabi Radishes	**Root vegetables** Beetroot Carrots Jerusalem artichokes Parsnips Potatoes Salsify Swedes Turnips
	Add manure or compost in autumn or early winter; add lime only if on acid soil	*Add lime in autumn or early winter unless on alkaline soil. Add manure 3 weeks later*	*Do not add manure, compost or lime*
YEAR 2	**Brassicas**	**Root vegetables**	**Legumes**
YEAR 3	**Root vegetables**	**Legumes**	**Brassicas**

Don't forget

As well as these temporary beds you will also need to include a permanent bed, or beds, for asparagus, globe artichokes and herbs, and a nursery bed or seed bed (see pages 28–9).

Seed-sowing and planting

With the notable exception of potatoes, onions and asparagus, the majority of vegetables tend to be grown from seed. Hardy vegetables, such as broad beans, are usually sown directly into the soil, while tender ones, like courgettes, are started off in pots under cover. Apart from melons, fruit is commonly bought as plants. Herbs are also usually bought as plants, although some, for example parsley and basil, can be raised from seed, either in pots or sown direct into the soil.

Direct sowing

Vegetables are generally sown in neat, evenly spaced rows, so that they can be distinguished from the weeds that inevitably grow around them. Rows also make hoeing and intercropping (see page 32) easier.

Preparing a seed bed

Before sowing seed, lightly fork over the soil and remove any weeds, then use a parallel-toothed garden rake to flatten and smooth the surface, getting rid of larger stones and breaking up clods of earth. You'll probably need to do this a couple of times in each direction until you end up with a 5–8cm (2–3in) depth of fine soil, which will allow even the smallest of vegetable seeds to grow through it.

To ensure straight rows, use pegs and string as a guide, or sow alongside a plank of wood. Small seeds are sprinkled into shallow furrows made with a trowel, a piece of bamboo or a hoe (see left). Large seeds can simply be pushed gently into the soil to the correct depth. They can easily be sown at the recommended spacings, while with

Fine seed is difficult to sow thinly, which makes thinning the resulting seedlings vital for a good crop.

smaller seeds you will need to do some thinning (see below left). Some trowels have measurements marked on their blades, or you can use a marked-up wooden batten to ensure your spacing is reasonably accurate.

Thinning

Once your seeds have germinated, it will become clear where seedlings are overcrowded, and some of these must be removed so that the rest can develop properly and provide you with a good crop. Working carefully down each row, pull out weak and damaged seedlings first, then healthy ones too, if necessary. Repeat thinning a few times as the plants grow; don't thin to the

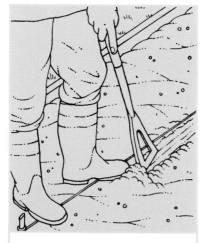

Before sowing seeds, mark out each seed row using a length of string tied to two canes. Stand on the line to keep it taut and use the corner of a hoe to make a shallow groove or 'drill' in which to plant the seeds.

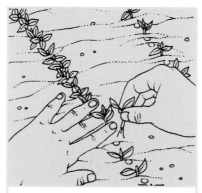

Thinning is important if you want to ensure a good, strong crop. Place your fingers on the soil on either side of the seedling that is to be removed to prevent neighbouring seedlings coming with it when you pull.

Don't forget

Cover the ground with horticultural fleece or black plastic to warm it up prior to planting.

recommended distances until you're sure each plant you leave is healthy enough to survive.

Protecting seedlings

Many young seedlings benefit from being covered with a cloche or piece of horticultural fleece in their young days (*see* pages 37–8). These will create a good, stable environment protected from excessive wind, wet and cold as well as birds and some insect pests. Don't forget to water regularly beneath such protection and, in the case of fleece, remove it fairly early on to prevent the foliage being damaged. You could also make a low frame with bamboo canes or something similar to lift the cover off the plants as they grow.

Sowing under cover

Plants like courgettes, sweetcorn and tomatoes, as well as melons, need a long growing season but are too tender to sow into the cold spring soil. They must be sown in pots or seed trays and grown to a reasonable size before planting out. You can raise them on a sunny

Some vegetables are best started in pots. With larger seeds, such as beans, plant just two per pot.

windowsill or in your conservatory. A heated propagator (*see* box, page 30) comes in useful but is not vital for most seeds. If you are more ambitious, invest in a greenhouse; it will transform your gardening.

With large seeds, sow two to a pot and either separate them into two pots soon after they germinate or remove the weaker of the two seedlings. With small seeds, scatter them thinly in seed trays and then prick them out into individual pots when they have two 'true' leaves ('seed' leaves are the first two to appear, followed by the 'true' leaves). Once sown, cover the seed with a thin layer of compost.

Nursery beds

Winter vegetables, such as sprouting broccoli, cabbages and leeks, are often raised in nursery beds, where they can be sown quite densely. Once they reach about 15–20cm (6–8in) high, they must be dug up – be careful not to damage the roots – and planted at their recommended spacings in the beds where they are to crop.

Tunnel cloches give young plants a protected environment that enables them to grow strongly without being damaged by adverse weather.

HOW TO prick out seedlings

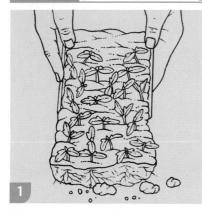

1

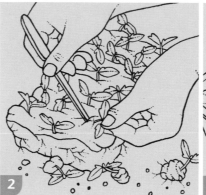

2

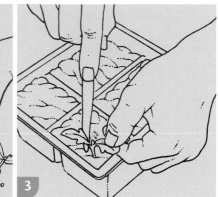

3

When young seedlings in seed trays or pots have two 'true' leaves, they can be pricked out into larger containers. Water the plants about an hour beforehand. Ease out the contents of the tray or pot onto a potting bench or other surface.

Using a plant label or a dibber, carefully separate individuals from the group. Hold them by the seed leaves, which have now served their purpose, never by their stems, and ease the roots out of the mass as gently as possible.

Plant the seedlings individually into pots or modules of compost. Gently firm the compost around their roots and water them in well. Protect the seedlings from high temperatures and bright light for a few days until they are established.

Propagators

Propagators can be heated or unheated – both types will increase your chances of success with a range of seeds. Unheated propagators are very inexpensive, although you can make your own with polythene bags or old plastic food containers. Heated propagators are more costly, but they're well worth the outlay, because they create a stable, warm environment, which really encourages some seeds, including tomatoes and melons, to germinate. You'll need to keep propagators at home, because you should check them daily; also, heated ones require electricity.

Always use good-quality loamless (soilless) potting compost and water with tap water, since water from a water butt may encourage fungal diseases such as damping off.

Hardening off and planting out seedlings

When the risk of frost has passed, plant out young seedlings into their final growing positions. First, harden them off carefully. This is where a cold frame comes in useful (*see* below and page 38). Put the plants into the cold frame. To start with, open the lid during the day and close it at night. After about a week, remove the lid, leaving it off unless poor weather is forecast. At the end of two or three weeks, they will be tough enough to plant out into the allotment. Fork over the soil, make a hole for each seedling and put it in place. Backfill with soil around the roots, firm it in gently and water well.

Don't forget

Garden centres often sell young vegetable plants. If you want only one or two chillies or tomatoes, these are good value and may give you the opportunity to try a range of varieties.

Cold frames are invaluable for helping young plants make the transition from the soft life under cover to the much tougher world outdoors.

Buying and planting fruit

Fruit will need a permanent position in the allotment, so the trees and bushes are best planted together, in a place where they won't cast shade on your vegetables and where they won't be disturbed by you digging around them.

Most fruit is sold in pots, but some, including apple trees and strawberries, are also sold as bare-root plants in autumn, when they're dormant. The advantage of bare-root plants is that they're less costly than pot-grown ones, and you often get a greater choice of varieties.

Unless you're buying by mail order, check plants thoroughly before purchase. You're looking for healthy, well-grown specimens with an even distribution of branches and, in the case of fruit trees, a straight trunk. If possible, ease the plant out of its container to make sure that it's not pot bound – if the roots are highly congested, filling the pot, it means that the plant is very likely to be 'stressed', making it unhealthy and slow to settle in and grow.

Don't forget

On an allotment, where space is tight, it is advisable to choose trees grown on a dwarf or semi-dwarfing rootstock (see page 82).

Mycorrhizal fungi

Fungi in the soil form a beneficial partnership with the roots of plants, helping them to take up nutrients and increasing their water supply. This takes several years if left to happen naturally, but you can buy these mycorrhizal fungi in a packet, in the form of granules, and use them when planting to get your plants off to a very good start. They are recommended for a range of permanent plants, including fruit trees and bushes.

It takes very little effort to persuade redcurrants to produce abundant crops of attractive berries.

Dwarf fruit trees, such as this pear (with a pheromone trap), can be maintained without using a ladder.

You can plant pot-grown fruit at more or less any time. Planting from autumn to spring is recommended, and if you plant in summer you'll need to water regularly. Bare-root plants must be planted immediately.

Once planted, tree fruit will need a firm stake for the first couple of years; after planting, hammer in a stake of about 1–1.2m (3–4ft) long, taking care to avoid the rootball, and attach the stake to the tree with a tree tie. In the case of pot-grown trees, angle the stake at 45 degrees to the ground, with the top facing in the direction of the prevailing wind; use a vertical stake for bare-root trees.

Cane fruit, for example raspberries and blackberries, require a system of posts and wires (*see* pages 36–7). Bushes, including blackcurrants and gooseberries, are usually pruned after planting (*see* page 41).

Ready-trained stepovers are good for edging beds and bear lots of low-level crops of normal-sized apples.

Vegetable growers usually make use of three types of intensive growing systems: intercropping, catch cropping and successional sowing. These are all methods to work every last inch of your plot throughout the year. They also help you to produce as much food as possible while avoiding gluts, which can result in having to discard perfectly good-quality fruit or vegetables because you can't keep up with production, or endless freezing and preserving (*see* page 43).

Make every inch of your plot count through intensive cropping.

① Squeeze salad leaves between rows of potatoes.

② By the time these young leeks need more space, the courgettes will have died down.

③ Peas are among the best crops for successional sowing.

Intercropping

Intercropping is when you sow a row or two of fast-growing vegetables between slower-growing plants. The intercrop will be ready to be harvested in just a few weeks, before the longer-term crop takes over the space and long before it matures.

Even if you start them off in nursery beds, brassicas – for example sprouting broccoli, cauliflowers and Brussels sprouts – go into their final positions in early or midsummer and remain there until late winter and early spring. This is a long time to have a piece of ground tied up. However, because they are slow-growing and, at least initially,

don't cast a great deal of shade, you can put a variety of fast-growing, short-term crops in around them (*see* box, below left). Just be careful not to disturb the ground too much when you harvest, because brassicas need to have firm soil around their roots.

Catch cropping

The idea behind catch cropping is quite similar to intercropping, but it is usually done to make use of empty ground at the beginning and end of the main growing season. Again, you sow fast-growing crops, but this time they're on their own rather than in between other crops.

In early spring, winter vegetables, such as winter-hearting cabbages and Brussels sprouts, are coming to an end.

As you harvest them and clear the ground, you can sow a quick crop of fast-growing vegetables to make use of the space before the summer residents are ready to go in. At this time of the year, use cloches to help early plants along. It's a good idea to start plants off indoors, too, if you have the space.

In autumn, as summer vegetables are coming to an end, you can again sow rows of fast-growing crops, which will mature before you need to put in overwintering vegetables, for instance broad beans, garlic, cabbages and kale.

Successional sowing

Successional sowing means staggering your seed-sowing over several weeks throughout the growing season. This ensures you have crops such as peas, beetroot and broad beans reaching harvesting stage over several weeks, not all at once. Successional sowing also acts like an insurance policy, because good growing weather cannot be guaranteed, especially in early spring. Crops like peas need reasonable warmth to germinate and grow away quickly to avoid being devastated by slugs and other pests. By sowing a row or two every week or so, you will be sure to have some vegetables to harvest. If any rows fail, simply resow.

Fast-growing crops

Radishes	Baby beetroot
Salad leaves	Baby carrots
Spinach	Baby turnips

Don't forget

To get the most out of your plot, devise a planting calendar. Make notes about what to sow and when (see opposite) to make sure you don't miss anything out.

Sowing, planting and harvesting timetable

This is a guide to the growing and harvesting periods of the vegetables in this book. Times may be affected by local weather conditions and you'll need to check the individual seed packets for specific details. 'Sow under cover' means sow indoors or in a covered seed bed. 'Sow outdoors' means sow *in situ* or in a seed bed. 'Plant' refers to planting into the cropping site, including pots or growing bags. It includes plants raised under cover or in seed beds, and bulbs and tubers. For more information, *see* pages 50–79.   *Good for sowing in succession*

VEGETABLE		SOW UNDER COVER	SOW OUTDOORS	PLANT	HARVEST
Artichokes, globe		March	April	April	July–September
Artichokes, Jerusalem		-	-	February–March	October–March
Asparagus		-	-	April	April–June
Aubergines		February–April	-	June	July–September
Beans, broad*		February–March	March–April, November	April	June–July
Beans, French*		April	May–June (dwarf varieties until July)	May	June–September (dwarf*), June–August (climbing*), September–October (flageolet, haricot)
Beans, runner		April	May	June	July–October
Beetroot*		March	April–June	-	June–October
Broccoli, sprouting		-	April–May	June–July	January–March
Brussels sprouts		February–March	March–April	May–June	September–March
Cabbages	Spring-hearting	-	July–August	September–October	April–May
	Summer- and autumn-hearting and red	March	April	May–June	August–October
	Winter-hearting and Savoy	-	April–May	June	November–February
Calabrese*		March	April–May	April–June	June–September
Carrots (early varieties)*		March	July–August	-	June–July, October–November
Cauliflowers	Summer-heading	January–February	-	March–April	May–July
	Autumn-heading	March	-	April–May	August–November
	Winter-heading	-	April–May	May–June	February–April
Celeriac		March	-	May–June	September–March
Celery (self-blanching)		March	-	May–June	August–October
Chicory*		-	June–July	-	October–December
Chillies		February–March	-	May–June	July–September
Courgettes, marrows, summer squashes		April	-	May–June	June–October
Cucumbers (outdoor)		April–May	-	May–June	July–September
Endive*		-	May–July	-	September–March
Florence fennel		May	-	June–July	August–September
Garlic		-	-	February–March, November	June–August
Kale		April	May–June	May–June	December–April
Kohl rabi*		-	April–June	-	July–September
Leeks		-	March–April	June	September–March
Lettuce and various salad leaves		March–April, October	April–September	April–May	April–November
Onions	Spring onions*	-	March–October	-	February–September
	Bulb (summer, sets)	-	-	March–April	August–September
	Bulb (overwintering, sets)	-	-	September–October	May–July
Parsnips*		-	March	-	July–December
Peas	Early*	February	March–April, June–July	April	June–July, September–October
	Maincrop*	-	April–July	-	July–September
	Mangetouts/sugar snaps*	-	April–June	-	June–September
Peppers		February–March	-	May–June	June–September
Potatoes	First earlies	February–March (chit)	-	March–April	May–July
	Second earlies	February–March (chit)	-	April	June–September
	Maincrop	-	-	April	September–November
Radishes	Summer	-	March–August	-	May–September
	Winter	-	July	-	August–November
Shallots (sets)		-	-	February–March	July–August
Spinach	Summer*	-	March–May	-	April–July
	Autumn*	-	August–October	-	September–November
Spinach, perpetual		-	April–July	-	July–October
Squashes and pumpkins		April	-	May–June	August–October
Swedes		-	May–June	-	September–February
Sweetcorn		April	-	May–June	July–September
Swiss chard		-	April–July	-	July–October
Tomatoes		March	-	May–June	August–September
Turnips*		-	April–July	-	June–September

Looking after plants

Once your precious plants are in the ground and growing away strongly, they'll need some regular care and attention to ensure that they continue to do well and produce a good crop. The work involved with growing both fruit and vegetables is much the same: watering, feeding and weeding as well as providing protection and support. You'll also need to keep an eye open for any pests and diseases (*see* pages 44–7).

Watering

For high yields you need to ensure your plants get lots of water. Spend time really soaking the ground around your crops – the water needs to reach the roots. Use your trowel to check how deep the water has gone – it can be surprising how much you need just to get down an inch or two.

Seeds

Vegetable seeds that have been sown directly into the soil in early spring should be able to fend for themselves to begin with, since they will begin to grow only when conditions are optimum, which includes the soil being damp. If the soil is very dry when you want to sow, it is worth watering it well beforehand – water gently into the drills – otherwise the seeds may sit there without germinating.

As the plants show their heads above the ground, you'll need to use your judgement on when to water. Long periods of dry weather slow plant growth and, if it is dry when the crop is forming, may result in low yields of tough vegetables.

When you water, give plants a good soaking to ensure that the water penetrates right down to the roots.

HOW TO earth up

This process involves covering plant stems with soil to block out light or frost. Earthing up potatoes and Jerusalem artichokes encourages shoots to root, which increases tuber production. With asparagus and celery it keeps the stems pale and tender.

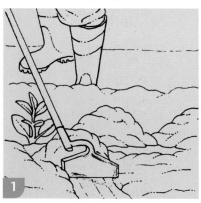

Plant the vegetable as normal. When the shoots start to appear, use a draw hoe or spade to bring soil up and over them so they get no light.

The shoots will reappear in a week or so. When they are about 15cm (6in) high, cover their lower half again. After this, leave the plants to develop normally.

Pot-raised plants

Once they're planted out, pot-raised vegetables, such as sweetcorn or courgettes, will need watering two or three times a week for the first couple of weeks until you're sure they've put down roots. Water them thoroughly on planting, too. If the soil is dry, you should water the planting hole beforehand.

Plants from nursery beds need even more help, since their roots get damaged in the move. Don't panic if you notice them wilting by the end of the day, even when well watered; they will gradually put down new roots and this will stop.

Don't forget

It is much more useful to your plants to water plentifully once a week than to give them a daily splash.

Fruit trees and bushes need to be watered regularly from the time they're planted until they're well established, which means more or less weekly for the first spring and summer. If you plant in the autumn, regular watering is less necessary, as the roots will have grown deeper down into the soil to find their own reserves by the time the plants begin to need water in the spring.

Feeding
Vegetable plants are very hungry and they need a regular, generous supply of food. Before planting, you should add humus-rich materials, such as compost, and slow-release fertilizers to the soil (see pages 24–6). During the growing season, you need to give them a boost with liquid or soluble feeds.

Foods for cropping plants
Fertilizers that are used to improve crops are usually soluble. They are either watered directly into the soil or sprayed on the leaves as a 'foliar feed' and are absorbed fairly rapidly. However, because they are soluble they will wash out of the soil and off leaves quickly too, which means you need to apply them regularly – once a week for tomatoes, for example.

Two very popular soluble fertilizers are tomato food and seaweed

Tomato feed is a nutritious food for a wide range of vegetables.

extract. Although it is called 'tomato food', this type of fertilizer will do a good job of feeding a wide range of plants, because it is a good source of potassium (K), which boosts flower and fruit production.

There are some organic feeds available, although they are more expensive. Seaweed makes a good foliar feed and is high in nitrogen (N). You can also make your own feed from plants (see box, below).

Weeding
No matter how well you've prepared your soil, weeds will appear. Weeds often grow very fast in carefully prepared soil, robbing your precious plants of food and water. They can also harbour diseases, such as rusts

and viruses, as well as making good hiding places for pests including slugs. They either produce masses of seeds or spread by roots and runners, multiplying very quickly and suffocating your seedlings.

Controlling weeds
The best way to control annual weeds among vegetables, most herbs and smaller fruit plants is to hoe off the weeds as soon as they appear, using a good hoe with a sharp blade that separates the roots from the top-growth (see page 19). Alternatively, you can try pulling them out whole, which is easy enough when they're in well-dug soil. The hand-pulling method is best around shallow-rooted plants, for example strawberries, as it less likely to damage the roots.

Don't forget
Ideally, hoe when the weather is dry so that the weeds die quickly. In wet weather, you'll need to remove them from the surface after hoeing in order to prevent regrowth.

Keep on top of weeds to stop them from encroaching on your plants and taking their food and water.

Making your own organic feed
You might want to try making your own liquid feeds from plants including borage, comfrey and stinging nettles. They are a good source of potassium (K) and nitrogen (N). Cultivate borage and comfrey on a spare patch of your allotment; stinging nettles might be available around the allotment site.

Gather the leaves and put them into a fine-mesh sack, which you immerse in water. Leave to rot. After a few weeks you can start to use the resulting dark, smelly liquid. Dilute it to look like weak tea and use as you would other liquid feeds. You may need to supplement home-made feeds with balanced fertilizers every so often.

Sturdy supports are vital for healthy, undamaged crops. Here, broad beans (shown on the left) are among many well-supported plants.

Whichever method you choose, be careful that you don't disturb young seedlings in the process.

Larger perennial weeds need to be dug out, because their roots will keep sprouting if left in the soil. Dig out as much of the root as possible, and check each time you tend the plants, removing any regrowth. You can also use a spot killer (most are based on glyphosate, *see* pages 21–2), but you must be very careful not to contaminate your plants.

You can keep the soil clear around fruit trees and bushes, as well as permanent herbs, such as rosemary, by digging out or hoeing.

Supporting plants

Although many vegetable plants are self-supporting, there are a few that must have something to grow on. Supports prevent the plants' stems from being damaged, as well as keeping the crop away from the soil, which means it stays clean, doesn't

rot and is safe from pests, including slugs. For the same reasons, fruit such as raspberries and kiwis need a good, strong system of permanent supports, while freestanding fruit trees need to be staked for the first couple of years until their roots have become well established.

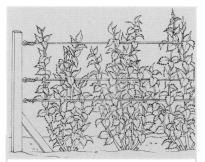

Post-and-wire fences make suitable supports for raspberries and other cane fruit. Tie the stems to the wires, spacing them out for easy harvesting.

Peasticks and canes

Peasticks are any twiggy branches that can be pushed into the soil for sprawling plants, such as peas, to scramble up or taller broad beans to lean on; prunings from fruit plants or deciduous hedges are ideal.

Bamboo canes or long hazel sticks are needed for taller plants, for example runner beans and climbing French beans, which often grow over 2m (6ft). They can be arranged either in a wigwam or in a row. Put the canes in place before planting and give the plants a helping hand to make their first few twists around the poles, tying them in place if necessary. They'll quickly get the idea and are self-clinging.

Don't forget

Sticks and canes need to be secure. Push the ends deeply into the ground.

Stakes

Staking plants, from tomatoes to raspberries and fruit trees, requires a variety of sturdy poles or tree stakes. A developing truss of tomatoes can be surprisingly heavy, and the branches are relatively weak, so choose a reasonably strong pole for them. Tie the plant to the stake with soft gardener's twine. Add ties as it grows to prevent the stems breaking under the weight of the fruit.

Raspberries and other cane fruit are often supported with a system of posts and wires (*see* opposite). Use posts set at intervals of about 4m (13ft). Screw vine-eyes into the posts and run wire through them. It's important that the wires are fixed firmly into place.

Fruit trees must be staked as soon as they're planted (*see* page 31).

Improvised protection

One of the best things about being on an allotment is that you get so many ideas from what other allotment-holders are doing. Making something useful out of stuff that other people throw away is a key part of being an allotmenteer. Old DVDs and CDs double up as bird scarers. Clear plastic water bottles can be used as individual cloches – just cut off the bases and remove the caps. Bricks and blocks can be used to prop up old windows as *impromptu* cold frames, while lengths of alkathene pipe can be bent into arches and covered in plastic sheeting to make tunnel cloches.

Mulching

If you're gardening in a very low rainfall area, it's well worth mulching over the soil surface after you have watered to reduce evaporation, particularly around fruit plants. You can use well-rotted compost or bark chippings and these will eventually feed the soil too. Mulching will also help to reduce weed growth.

Leave the stake in place for the first two years or so, and check tree ties on a regular basis, loosening them as the tree trunk grows.

Protecting plants

To ensure you get large crops of unblemished, juicy fruit and succulent, tender vegetables, you may need to provide them with protection during some or all of their lives. Plants such as tomatoes, aubergines and peppers perform much better if they're given a permanently warm spot, with shelter from cold winds and lashing rain, while developing strawberries need to be lifted away from the soil to prevent rotting. Other plants are quite hardy, but benefit from a bit of warmth when young. There are also animal pests to consider, particularly rabbits and birds, who will eat your crops if you let them.

Rabbit-proof fencing

If you have animal pests on your allotment, you'll need to take quite drastic measures to keep them away from your crop. The only practical way to keep rabbits off is to put up sturdy chicken-wire fences.

You'll need to bury the fence at least 15cm (6in) deep, but for the most satisfactory results make it 30cm (12in) deep with a 45-degree outward bend (like an open L-shape) in the lower 15cm (6in) to prevent the rabbits digging under it. The fence should be 90–120cm (3–4ft)

Tunnel cloches with fine-mesh netting or plastic sheeting protect plants from pests and poor weather.

high, because rabbits can jump. The mesh should be no larger than 2.5cm (1in) to keep out baby rabbits. Secure the chicken wire in place by stapling it onto strong posts.

Windbreaks

Cold winds come from the north and east, but most of the wet and windy weather comes from the south west. If your allotment is very exposed, you can reduce the effect of inclement weather by putting up windbreak meshes on the most exposed side. Make sure you use strong posts to support them. If you prefer something more attractive, there are bamboo or rush screens; you could even erect trellis or low fencing, as long as these are allowed on your allotment. Windbreaks may be costly and time-consuming to install, but if they save your crops they will be well worthwhile.

Fleece

Horticultural fleece is a soft, light, white fabric that you drape over seedlings and young plants to protect them from the worst of the weather, making it possible to get earlier and later crops. It can also be used to prevent airborne pests, for

Polytunnels and greenhouses

If you have the space and can afford to buy one (or find one second hand), a polytunnel or greenhouse will transform your fruit and vegetable gardening. Crops such as chillies, tomatoes, cucumbers, peppers and aubergines all do so much better under cover. With this type of spacious protection, it is easier to start seedlings and to grow early and late crops of vegetables, including lettuces, salad leaves, French beans and beetroot, while pots of strawberries will provide you with a supply several weeks before outdoor plants start to fruit.

example carrot fly and cabbage white butterflies, laying eggs on your crops, and birds pecking your strawberries. It is light enough just to drape over the top of crops, or you can make low frames from bamboo canes and tie it to these.

Mats and straw

Strawberries need to be lifted off the soil before they start to ripen so that they stay clean and dry; if they get wet, they can rot. Traditionally, straw is used and is simply eased in under the strawberries. However, you can also buy strawberry mats, which are placed like collars around the plants, keeping weeds down as well as protecting the fruit. Mats are

also useful for preventing cabbage root flies from reaching the roots of cabbages and other brassicas. Pieces of cardboard or old wool carpet can also be used.

Cloches

Cloches are among the most useful items to have on your allotment. They come in a variety of designs, depending on what you want to use them for: long and narrow for protecting rows of crops, or round or square to cover individual plants. Waterproof cloches are most commonly used to create warm, sheltered microclimates, which encourage fast growth. They are usually made of plastic and you'll need to water underneath them.

Don't forget

You should always remove the netting from the top of your fruit cage before winter sets in.

Use strawberry mats to protect the fruit from soil splashes, which can cause rot, and slug damage.

Those made from netting (see page 37) are used to protect crops from birds and insect pests, but they will still improve growing conditions by providing shelter from wind and some rain.

Cold frames

Cold frames are the perfect halfway house for hardening off plants raised at home before planting out on the allotment (see page 30). You could also plant them straight out and use a cloche to protect them, but hardening off gradually is more likely to be successful. You can buy cold frames relatively cheaply, or make your own in true allotment tradition using bricks or wooden planks and old windows. Inside the frame, a weedproof membrane thickly covered with gravel makes a good base to stand plant pots on.

Fruit cages

If you're growing lots of fruit, it makes good sense to erect a fruit cage around the plants, which will keep them safe from birds. Choose a cage with a robust frame that is easy to anchor firmly and has a mesh large enough to allow in pollinating insects.

Fruit cages can be pricey, so you might like to make one. Construct a frame with wooden stakes and staple or tie the netting to it. A cage for strawberries need only be 60cm (24in) or so high – you can move it aside when you want to get at the strawberries – but for other fruit it is better to construct one that you can walk upright in, as this makes tending the plants and harvesting the fruit easy and comfortable.

Pruning

If you're going to grow fruit well you'll need to prune, but don't let that put you off – it's pretty straightforward really. Pruning keeps plants healthy by removing dead, diseased and damaged stems. It also manages growth, ensuring stems and branches are able to support a crop and altering the balance between the roots and the top-growth, which encourages fruit production.

Pruning fruit trees and bushes after the leaves have fallen allows you to see the plant's overall shape.

The basics

Pruning is mainly done in autumn or winter, with some tidying up in spring and summer. It isn't always necessary – *see* the directory (pages 82–93) for the individual needs of each type of fruit. Before you start, ensure you have the right tools and understand where and how to cut.

Pruning tools

Always buy good-quality pruning tools that have sharp blades and comfortable handles. Whatever fruit you grow, you'll need the following:

Secateurs These can cut stems up to 1cm (½in) thick. Anvil secateurs have a sharp blade that closes on a flat edge, while bypass secateurs are scissor-like in their action. Bypass secateurs are the best choice for hollow or brittle stems.

Pruning saw This is needed for cutting branches that are too thick for secateurs. Those with double-edged blades are more versatile: the fine teeth are good for dead wood, while the coarse ones make light work of sappy wood.

Loppers Like secateurs, these long-handled pruners have either bypass or anvil blades. They are good for branches 1–2.5cm (½–1in) thick, particularly for ones that are out of reach.

Where and how to cut

Always make clean, neat cuts with sharp tools just above a healthy-looking bud. The buds are where the

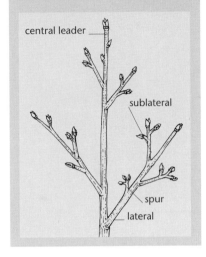

growth is concentrated, so cuts here will heal more quickly. The bud will soon burst into life and grow away in the direction in which it is pointing, so choose a bud that will go in the desired direction – this is usually outwards from the centre of the plant. Where the buds are opposite each other, make a cut straight across the stem; where they are staggered (alternate), make a sloping cut of about 25 degrees.

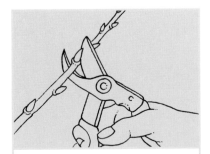

An angled cut above an alternate bud

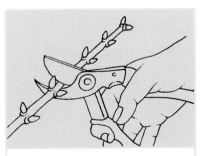

A straight cut above opposite buds

Cordon apples are pruned annually to reduce the number of fruiting spurs for maximum fruit production.

Pruning fruit trees

Established freestanding apples and pears do not need much pruning. Supported trees, such as cordons, require a lot more. Freestanding plum trees are best unpruned, but if necessary they can be pruned in late spring or summer; never do it in winter (see page 90).

Freestanding trees

The most suitable freestanding fruit trees for an allotment are bushes or half-standards. These are grown on

Don't forget

Fruit trees can also be grown as espaliers and fans against a shed wall. As well as saving space, the advantages of growing trees this way is that the wall retains heat and provides shelter from the worst of the weather.

special rootstocks that keep them relatively small (see page 82). Both have a short trunk – longer on a half-standard – with branches radiating from the top. They produce plenty of fruit and are easy to prune (see box, below).

Cordons

Cordons growing on wires are an option where space is at a premium. They can be planted individually or several can be positioned 45–90cm (18–36in) apart to form a 'hedge'. For maximum fruit production, cordons are best planted and trained at an angle of 45 degrees, with the main stem tied to a cane, which is attached to a framework of wires.

The first year After planting the cordon, or in the first winter, prune laterals over 10cm (4in) to four buds; cut just above an outward-facing bud. The following summer, prune new growth to three leaves and sublaterals to one leaf – this creates the fruiting spurs.

Subsequent years In the second winter, and every winter thereafter, thin any crowded fruiting spurs. When the leader reaches the top wire, trim its new growth back to one leaf in spring. In summer, prune both new and mature laterals to three leaves and all sublaterals to one leaf. This keeps growth compact and encourages fruiting spurs.

Pruning established apples and pears

Most apples and pears carry their fruit in clusters on short branches (spurs) that are at least two years old (see below left). However, some produce most of their fruit on the tips of last year's growth (see below right). Both types are pruned in winter, but the techniques differ.

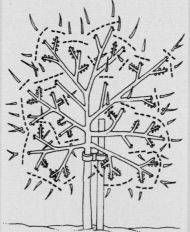

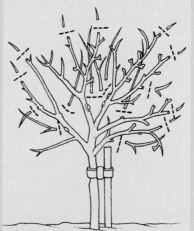

SPUR-BEARING TREES
Cut back the end third of each lateral. Prune back new sublaterals on the rest of the framework to five buds, to encourage more fruiting spurs to form. Thin out overcrowded, old or weak spurs and any that develop on the underside of the main branches.

TIP-BEARING TREES
Remove a quarter of the oldest fruiting branches, thinning out the centre of the tree (eventually, the whole of the top-growth will be replaced). Shorten just the tips of the remaining branches. Cut out any water shoots (fast-growing straight stems).

Pruning soft-fruit bushes

When it comes to pruning soft-fruit bushes, there are two main methods: one is used for blackcurrants and jostaberries, and the other for the remaining currants and gooseberries (*see* box, right). When pruning, do remember to remove dead, damaged and weak stems. Crowded stems may be cut out or shortened.

Blackcurrants and jostaberries

The youngest blackcurrant stems produce the most fruit, so pruning concentrates on removing a few of the oldest, least-productive stems each year. Always cut the stems as close to the base of the plant as possible, and evenly around the bush so it looks balanced with well-spaced stems when you're finished.

The first year In spring (just as the buds start to swell), or soon after planting, cut down all the stems to one healthy bud just above soil level. The following winter, cut out any damaged branches and reduce thin, weak or small shoots to just above ground level. Thin out any strong shoots that are growing too close together. (For established bushes, *see* box, top right.)

Other currants and gooseberries

Redcurrants, whitecurrants and gooseberries are grown as small bushes on a single, short 'leg' and

> ### Don't forget
> When pruning, always cut to a plump, undamaged bud, even if it means taking off a little more than you planned, as healthy buds are more likely to develop into strong shoots.

Pruning established soft-fruit bushes

Blackcurrants produce many stems at ground level, while redcurrants, whitecurrants and gooseberries usually grow from a short stem, or 'leg'. They are pruned differently.

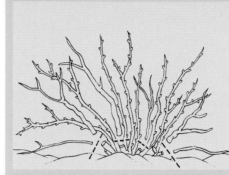

BLACKCURRANTS

Each winter (or after harvest), remove a few of the oldest fruit-bearing stems, cutting as close to the ground as possible, or to just above a strong new shoot low down on the bush. Aim to remove about one third of the growth evenly from all around the plant.

OTHER CURRANTS AND GOOSEBERRIES

Each late winter or early spring, reduce overcrowded or crossing stems to about 2cm (¾in) long and remove a few older laterals, shortening the rest by a quarter. In summer, cut sublaterals to a finger's length and thin out some of the new growth.

they bear fruit on short spurs that grow from the laterals. Two- or three-year-old laterals are the most prolific, so pruning is carried out to encourage new laterals and lots of spurs as well as removing older laterals and any that develop in the 'leg' area. The aim is also to keep the centre of the bush open, which makes picking easier and allows for air circulation. An established bush will have between nine and twelve fruiting laterals.

The first year On planting or in the first winter, create the 'leg' by removing all lateral growth up to 20cm (8in) above the ground. Select about six healthy laterals to form the basis of the bush and prune these to half of their length. Remove all the other laterals. The next winter, cut back new growth all over the bush by half. Stems growing into the

centre can be cut to a single bud, which will encourage the spurs. (For established bushes, *see* box, above.)

Pruning canes

Cane fruit includes raspberries, blackberries and their relatives, and they produce their crops on many-stemmed, shapeless plants. They need pruning to keep the canes under control and to remove some of the older, less productive canes. All cane fruit requires supports of about 2m (6ft) tall (*see* pages 36–7).

There are two main techniques for pruning cane fruit. The first method covers raspberries and other canes with a similar stiff, upright growth, such as shorter upright blackberry varieties; the second method covers the more lax, arching blackberries as well as closely related plants, including loganberries, tayberries and boysenberries.

Pruning established cane fruit

For pruning purposes, cane fruit is divided into two main groups: plants that have upright, stiff, erect stems (e.g. raspberries and some upright blackberries) and those that have a lax habit, with long, trailing stems (e.g. most blackberries and their relatives).

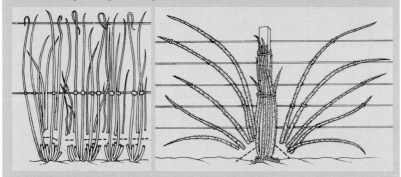

AUTUMN-FRUITING RASPBERRIES
In late winter or early spring, cut autumn-fruiting raspberries to 8cm (3in) above the ground. In early summer, remove shoots that are less than 1m (40in) high and thin out the remaining new shoots to 8–10cm (3–4in) apart to allow space for them to develop. Tie them to their supports.

BLACKBERRIES AND THEIR RELATIVES
Each year after harvesting lax-stemmed blackberries and their relatives, remove all the old canes that are on the wires, cutting close to ground level. Select the strongest canes from the central bundle and train them on the wires. In spring, tidy the canes, removing damaged shoot-tips.

Raspberries and similar canes

After planting, remove weaker canes and tie the rest to the supports; this will encourage establishment and the growth of new canes.

There are two sorts of raspberries: summer-fruiting varieties and autumn-fruiting ones. With summer-fruiting varieties, pruning consists of removing old canes after they have fruited and cutting weak new canes to soil level. Tie the remaining new shoots to supports, spacing them as

No-prune raspberries

You can avoid summer pruning of autumn-fruiting raspberries. Cut all the shoots to 8cm (3in) above the ground in late winter or early spring, as shown (see box, above), but then don't worry about thinning out the new growth. So long as you feed and mulch well, you'll get a great crop as well as a thick hedge, which you'll only need to thin every few years.

evenly as possible. In late autumn, reduce taller canes so they protrude only about 15cm (6in) above the top of the support. (For autumn-fruiting varieties, see box, above and below.)

Blackberries and their relatives

After planting blackberries and similar canes, such as loganberries, tayberries and boysenberries, cut out all weak stems and reduce the strongest shoots to 25–30cm (10–12in) above the ground. This will result in strong new shoots from the base, which will need tying in as they grow. When they reach 2m (6ft) or more long, remove the end 15cm (6in) in order to encourage fruiting laterals.

One of the easiest ways to grow blackberries is in a fan shape. Established canes are trained along wires and as new canes grow

through the season, they are tied to a central support to keep them separate (see box, left).

Pruning vines

The rod-and-spur method is one of the simplest ways to grow grapes and kiwis and is suitable for training them on fences, trellis and similar supports. The technique varies slightly between the two. In both cases, begin by tying the main stem (rod) to a vertical support. Select two strong laterals from near the base of the rod and tie these onto horizontal supports. With kiwis, you can allow additional sideshoots to develop about every 30cm (12in) up the rod to the top of the support.

Grapes

In summer, stems will grow from the vine's horizontal laterals. Choose three or four sublaterals that are growing vertically from each lateral and tie them to your support. They will produce spurs, which will flower and then bear fruit. Allow these to develop about every 30cm (12in). When they flower, trim spurs back to two leaves beyond the cluster; trim spurs without flowers to five or six leaves in all. Each winter, reduce the spurs to two buds, allowing one of these to develop the next summer.

Kiwis

In summer, the horizontal laterals will produce sublaterals. You want these to be about 50cm (20in) apart, so remove any in between. Clip the sublaterals, leaving five or six leaves. This will encourage them to produce spurs, which will carry the fruit.

It stands to reason that most fruit and vegetables taste best straight from the allotment, with as little time as possible between picking and eating. However, some plants, such as onions, are usually ready to be harvested in one go, while others, including broad beans, produce such vast quantities that it is impossible to eat them all when they're in their prime, even if you do sow them in succession (*see* page 32). The solution is storage.

In the shed

Onions and maincrop potatoes can be stored for many months in a cool, dry shed. This is also a good place for late-cropping apples and roots such as carrots and parsnips, although these are best left in the ground unless the weather is very wet, which might lead to rotting.

Store only unblemished fruit and vegetables and clean them well before packing them away. Use clean, dry boxes and shelving units. Onions need to be stored in a light area, while potatoes must be kept in the dark. Make sure you can easily access all your stored produce so that you can check it regularly for rot. Remove anything that looks like it is deteriorating. You might still be able to use some of it in cooking, but if you leave it where it is, it'll quickly affect its neighbours.

In the freezer

Soft fruit and a range of vegetables, including beans, peas and sweetcorn, can be frozen and will remain in a good condition in the freezer for several

When stored properly, fruit and vegetables keep for months.

① Tissue protects apples and slows the spread of any rot.

② Hessian sacks are ideal for potatoes, which need darkness.

③ Onions like a cool, light place; you can hang them up in bunches.

④ Thread chillies on string and hang them to dry.

⑤ Freeze broad beans on the day they are picked.

months. Wash and dry fruit before freezing; vegetables and rhubarb should be blanched, too. Spread them out in single layers on shallow trays to freeze, then put them into bags or plastic boxes afterwards.

Courgettes and tomatoes, along with crunchy fruit, like apples, and stone fruit, such as plums, are best cooked before freezing. Tomatoes can be baked in the oven with olive oil, basil and garlic, making a sauce that can be the basis for a range of dishes. Apple pies and crumbles are also suitable for freezing.

Making preserves

Jams and chutneys are the traditional method of storage and are a great way to deal with gluts of fruit that do not freeze well, such as strawberries. Tomatoes make wonderful chutneys and can be combined with many other ingredients, while chillies and onions are very easy to pickle. Most other fruit and vegetables can be used in preserves of one sort or another. There should be no reason to throw away excess produce, but if the worst comes to the worst, put it on the compost heap to feed next year's plants.

Plant problems and remedies

One of the most trying things about growing your own fruit and vegetables is that no matter how carefully you tend them, your plants will occasionally have problems. Looking after them properly will help them to resist attacks, but there will still be times when they succumb to pests and diseases. The best way to minimize damage is to keep your eyes skinned and take action as soon as you spot something going wrong.

Avoiding problems

It is far better to grow a few plants well than many rather badly. Make sure you observe recommended planting distances, since crowded plants are considerably more likely to be unhealthy. Make full use of protective coverings and support plants properly. Feed regularly but don't overfeed: lush growth will encourage pests, such as aphids, as well as reducing your crop. Water thoroughly and regularly. Prune fruit plants as recommended and make use of fruit cages. When pruning, keep your tools extremely clean to avoid spreading diseases from plant to plant; wipe the blades with methylated spirits if you're removing diseased wood.

Aphids

Aphids are tiny, green, black or pink insects. You'll find them in clusters around soft new growth or on the underside of leaves of a range of plants. They suck sap, causing distortion of the foliage and weakening the plant.
Prevention and control Cloches covered with fine mesh may prevent aphids reaching your plants, but put them in place very early in the year.

Use your thumb and finger to squash a small infestation. Be careful not to damage the growth. Check every few days for new hatchings. Try biological controls (*see* box, right). As a last resort, spray with an organic insecticide, but check it is suitable for edible plants.

Blight

This is a disease of potatoes and tomatoes. Yellow, then brown, blotches around the edges of the leaves quickly spread to the stems. Blight spreads through neighbouring related plants with equal speed and kills them within hours.
Prevention and control Burn or otherwise dispose of the diseased plants. Potatoes may have developed a crop, which will be fine for a while under the soil, but you must remove the top-growth immediately. It's best to prevent blight in the first place by fortnightly spraying with copper-based fungicide from mid- to late summer. Grow resistant varieties and choose early potatoes, because they will crop before blight's peak season, which is during early summer (especially in damp weather).

Make your plot attractive to beneficial insects, such as ladybirds. They'll help keep down numbers of insect pests.

Biological controls

Biological controls are microscopic creatures that attack common fruit and vegetable pests, but are harmless to the environment. They are available from specialist suppliers. Unfortunately, many are effective only in greenhouses or polytunnels. In the list below, the ant, aphid, codling moth and slug controls will work outdoors too. Combination controls for blanket use against a range of pests, including cabbage root fly and carrot fly, are also available.

PEST	BIOLOGICAL CONTROL
Ant	*Steinernema feltiae* (nematode)
Aphid	*Adalia bipunctata* (ladybird larvae or adults) and *Chrysopa carnea* (lacewing larvae)
Codling moth caterpillar and gooseberry sawfly larvae	*Steinernema carpocapsae* (nematode)
Red spider mite	*Phytosieulus persimilis* (predatory mite)
Slug	*Phasmarhabditis hermaphrodita* (nematode)
Vine weevil	*Steinernema kraussei* (nematode)
Whitefly	*Encarsia formosa* (parasitic wasp)

Botrytis (grey mould)

Yellowing or browning of the leaves, followed by white or grey 'felt', is a sign of botrytis, which flourishes in cool, damp, poorly ventilated conditions. It causes the white marks known as ghost spot on tomatoes and damages strawberries.

Prevention and control Increase air circulation as far as possible. Use strawberry mats to keep the fruit off the soil. Clear up all plant debris to avoid the spores overwintering.

Canker diseases

Various fungal diseases affect plums and related species, as well as apples. They usually appear as brown spots on the leaves (shothole disease). The following year, buds may fail and leaves may wither. Twigs and branches die, their bark damaged by oozing cankers.

Prevention and control Remove affected branches. Cut back to healthy wood. Spray smaller trees with copper-based fungicide in mid- and late summer. Sadly, there is no cure once the disease has spread throughout the tree.

Don't forget

An allotment site full of fruit and vegetables is a great target for a range of pests and diseases. Ask around to see what other allotment-holders have found to be the greatest problems and take preventative action against these if possible.

Caterpillars

Caterpillars are very destructive and attack a range of plants. In particular, cabbage white caterpillars eat brassicas, while winter moth caterpillars feed on the young growth of pears and plums. Sawfly larvae, which look quite similar, can shred gooseberry leaves.

Prevention and control Protect brassicas with fine-mesh cloches before you see cabbage white butterflies on the allotment. Pick off caterpillars on sight. Check under-sides of leaves and remove clusters of tiny eggs. Use grease or sticky strips (available from garden centres) around fruit tree trunks to reduce winter moth numbers. Try biological controls (*see* box, opposite).

Club root

Club root is a disease that can infect all brassicas, including cabbages, broccoli and Brussels sprouts. The roots swell and eventually rot, often becoming very smelly, and the top-growth is badly stunted.

Prevention and control The disease stays in the ground for 20 years or more, during which time you will not be able to grow any brassicas. There's no cure. Make sure you don't get it by raising all your own plants,

by growing brassicas in well-drained soil and by liming acid soil before planting (*see* page 25). The disease is less common on chalky, alkaline soils and where drainage is good.

Damping off

The sudden collapse and death of trays of seedlings is usually caused by this fungal disease, which enters the plant through the roots.

Prevention and control Sow seedlings thinly and ensure they have good air circulation. Prevent its appearance by watering with a copper-based fungicide. Use tap water, rather than water from a butt, which might harbour disease.

Fireblight

This is a bacterial disease of apples, pears and related species. It makes the shoots, flowers and leaves turn black and wilt. The stems may develop oozing cankers. The underlying tissues may be stained a foxy red colour.

Prevention and control Remove affected growth. Cut 30cm (12in) into healthy wood (scratch the bark to check for the staining) on stems and branches; double that on larger branches. Dig up and destroy smaller plants.

Leaf spots

Many fruit plants can develop spots on the leaves, but some soft fruit, such as black-currants (shown right) and gooseberries, are particularly prone to them.

Two of the most common spots on vegetables are chocolate spots on broad beans, which is caused by a fungal disease, and bean halo blight (shown right) on dwarf French beans and runner beans, caused by a bacterial disease in the seeds. (*See also* Canker diseases, Rusts, Powdery mildew and Viruses.)

Prevention and control As long as the plants are otherwise healthy, leaf spots shouldn't cause too much harm. However, it is worth clearing up and burning affected leaves in autumn to prevent any diseases from spreading. Mulch the soil around the plants to prevent the spores from splashing up in the rain. With broad beans, planting further apart in a well-ventilated spot should reduce problems. With runners and dwarf French beans, don't soak the seeds before planting and avoid wetting the leaves when you water. Use a copper-based fungicide spray as a preventative measure for fruit and one based on plant and fish oils for beans.

Powdery mildew

Powdery mildew first appears as a white powder on the surface of the leaves, which may also turn yellow and become rather thin-textured. Some plants, such as courgettes, will nearly always suffer from this fungal disease towards the end of the growing season.

Prevention and control Powdery mildew is often a sign of damp air conditions and dry roots, so water the soil rather than the whole plant. Increase air circulation around plants by spacing them more widely.

Red spider mite

These microscopic mites usually infest plants in very dry weather, making the leaves turn yellow and producing a dusty, webby growth on their undersides.

Prevention and control Water plants well and spray the air around them to increase humidity. Keep plants well watered to avoid the problem in the first place. Under cover, use a biological control (*see* box, page 44). For big infestations outdoors, use an organic pesticide approved for cropping plants.

Root flies

The maggot-like larvae of root flies damage some crops and may completely ruin them.

Carrot fly larvae make brown-stained tunnels on the outer surfaces of developing carrots, while onion fly larvae are often found on the lower surface of the bulb and the roots. Cabbage fly larvae eat the roots of cabbages and related plants.

Prevention and control Use barriers to prevent the flies laying their eggs near the plants. Horticultural fleece or fine-mesh netting can be laid over carrots and onions, while it is easier to make your own collars from cardboard, old wool carpet or any other similar material to put around cabbages. Onions grown from sets are less likely to suffer from damage.

Companion planting

The idea behind companion planting is that some plants, particularly strongly aromatic herbs, will distract pests from your crops, either because of their smell or through chemicals excreted by their roots. It is more widely practised with vegetables than fruit, and not everyone finds that it works, but it is well worth having a go.

Here are some planting suggestions:

- Basil with tomatoes to deter whitefly
- French marigolds (shown right with curly kale) anywhere to reduce numbers of soil pest nematodes, slugs and wireworms
- Nasturtiums to attract aphids from broad beans and cabbage white butterflies from brassicas
- Wormwood (*Artemisia*) or catmint (*Nepeta*) to deter flea beetles.

Rots

Rots can affect the crop as well as the plant. Brown rot is a fungal infection that produces brown areas and white concentric circles on apples, pears and plums. Buckeye rot is a similar problem in tomatoes. Bacterial soft rot is most common on root crops, causing discoloration and softening of the tissues, but you often don't notice it because the problem is under the ground.

Prevention and control Rots get in via broken skin and outer tissues, so avoid damaging plants and fruit. Practise good cultivation techniques and combat pests, such as aphids and root flies, which cause the initial damage. Pick off affected fruit to reduce spread.

Rusts

Rusts are fungal diseases that cause rust-like spots on the leaves. They can affect a range of plants, including beans (dark brown spots), leeks (bright orange), gooseberries (orange-red) and plums (brown leaf undersides). Plants may be weakened but you'll often still get a crop.

Prevention and control Space plants well. On gooseberries and beans, remove the affected parts. Don't overfeed leeks and use sulphate of potash when you plant them; grow resistant varieties. Feed plum trees and rake up leaves and mulch to limit reinfection.

Silver leaf

A serious disease of plums and related species, this is caused by a fungus that enters the tree through wounds in the bark. The leaves take on a silvery appearance before turning brown and dying. If you cut through an affected stem, you'll see a brown stain running through the centre.

Prevention and control Avoid pruning and if you must prune, do so in summer, when fewer fungal spores are in the air and the plant will heal more quickly. Cut back to healthy wood – at least 15cm (6in) beyond the end of the staining.

Slugs and snails

Notoriously destructive, especially of seedlings and young plants, slugs and snails are very likely to be responsible for any overnight disappearance of developing crops, as well as holes in strawberries, courgettes and beans.

Prevention and control Remove all plant debris, large stones and other potential hidey holes. Spend time searching out these pests and then dispatch them in a pot of salted water. Fix copper tape around raised beds and scatter absorbent granules, such as those made from wool, around your plants. Use a biological control (*see* box, page 44) to reduce numbers. As a last resort, use slug pellets based on aluminium sulphate or ferric phosphate.

Soil pests

Soil pests include cutworms (shown right), which cut through the base of plants, separating the roots from the stems, and wireworms (shown below), which are shiny, yellow-orange maggots that bore into root crops, such as potatoes. Lettuce root aphids feed on the roots of lettuces.

Prevention and control Practise crop rotation (*see* page 27) to avoid a build-up of problems. Soil pests are more prevalent in neglected allotments, so numbers should reduce in successive years.

Viruses

Virus diseases show up as mottling, marbling or yellowing of the foliage. They reduce the plant's vigour and affect the crop in a wide range of fruit and vegetables.

Prevention and control Keep aphids under control in order to prevent viruses spreading between crops. Remove weeds, because they can harbour viruses. Buy virus-free fruit plants in the first place. There is no treatment for viruses, so dig up and destroy affected plants.

Seasonal tasks

When you have an allotment, you're never short of something to do and you've never done everything you want to do. Even in the dead of winter, a fine day offers the opportunity for sprucing up the shed or building a new compost bin; in the summer, the long evenings can be filled with weeding, feeding, tying in and watering. Then come the rewards – the harvesting of your crops.

Runner beans crop prolifically, so long as they get plenty of water through the summer.

Early spring

■ Dig over the empty beds and scatter a slow-release fertilizer. If you didn't do it last autumn, add well-rotted, humus-rich material to most beds, except those that are going to contain root vegetables.
■ Top-dress fruit, water plants well, if necessary, and add a thick mulch.
■ Dig green manures into the soil.
■ Chit potatoes and sow or plant early batches of vegetables if you didn't do this in late winter.
■ Plant strawberries.

Mid-spring

■ Even in your first year, you can be harvesting early crops of salad leaves and spring onions. In subsequent years there will also be asparagus, cabbages and kale to enjoy, among many others.
■ Weed regularly to counteract the fast growth of weeds at this time of year. Make a note of any persistent perennial weeds, such as dandelions and bindweed, and cut off the top-growth on every visit. This will eventually kill them.
■ Watering may be necessary. Don't allow plants to go dry in spring.
■ Start hardening off tender plants. Use a cold frame and cover plants with fleece or a cloche when chilly weather is forecast.
■ Continue sowing seed and planting vegetables.
■ Plant blueberries for crops later this year.

Late spring

■ Among crops ready to be harvested are asparagus, spring-hearting cabbages, early potatoes, the first summer spinach leaves, culinary gooseberries and rhubarb.
■ In cold weather, protect tender vegetables with cloches or fleece.
■ Keep an eye open for pests, such as aphids. In damp weather, young slugs can be very destructive. Use a biological control (*see* page 44).
■ Start preparing for winter and early-spring crops by transplanting brassicas from their nursery bed to their cropping position.

Lettuces grow quickly and can be picked while still young. Sow successively from early spring for a continuous supply.

Early summer

■ Step up watering and feeding. Give many veg a weekly liquid feed.
■ Sow chicory for blanched 'chicons' in the autumn and winter.
■ Plant out runner beans and give them good, sturdy supports.
■ Plant melons and give them as much protection as possible.
■ Harvest second early potatoes, peas and garlic as well as salad crops and courgettes. Fruit to pick include gooseberries, strawberries and rhubarb.
■ Thin tree fruit.
■ If you have a greenhouse, put up shading materials to keep bright sunlight off your crops. This will also slow down water loss. Leave doors open as much as possible.

Midsummer

■ Harvest summer raspberries, redcurrants and whitecurrants.
■ Feed and water on a regular basis. Check the soil after rain. It may still be necessary to water.
■ Carry on sowing successional crops, including turnips. Now is also

a good time to put in early carrots, and it's not too late for a late sowing of dwarf French beans and peas (earlies and maincrops).

■ Keep an eye on tomato plants. Keep trimming off sideshoots of cordon varieties and check supports regularly – heavy fruit trusses can break stems.

■ Prune cordon and stepover fruit trees and kiwis, grapes, gooseberries and red- and whitecurrants.

■ Water butts are always empty when you most need water. If you run out of water now, make a note to install more water-saving containers as soon as possible.

Late summer

■ Keep on top of tomatoes. Remove the lower leaves to encourage them to put all their energy into ripening the fruit before the cool nights of early autumn put paid to the plants.

■ Put in a few more rows of salad leaves, carrots and radishes.

■ Prune summer-fruiting raspberries after you've picked all the fruit.

■ Keep on clipping back grapes and kiwi fruit – they grow very fast.

■ The fruit harvest begins in earnest, with apples, blackberries and even a few melons ripening towards the end of summer.

Early autumn

■ Get on top of digging and adding compost to beds for next year. Once they are prepared, cover the beds with black plastic sheet, weedproof membrane or thick cardboard to prevent weed regrowth.

■ Harvest your fruit, which will be abundant now, keeping you busy on the allotment and in the kitchen.

Gooseberries are tasty and versatile and need very little encouragement to produce a good crop.

■ Start pruning cane fruit, for example blackberries, after you've harvested the fruit.

■ Consider planting a green manure to boost fertility on beds that haven't performed as well as you'd like them to.

■ Finish off harvesting tomatoes, aubergines and cucumbers (in a good year, some may continue into mid-autumn) and put the dead or dying plants on the compost heap.

■ Cover late-sown salad crops with fleece or cloches in colder weather, to keep them going a bit longer.

Mid-autumn to late winter

■ Prepare permanent beds for fruit (bare-root trees are available only at this time of year) and plant them now so they have time to establish before cropping next year. Stake trees firmly.

Make the most of the autumn and winter months to improve your soil; it will encourage healthier crops.

■ Continue pruning fruit trees, bushes and canes. Tidy up prunings and burn them or put them out for council-run composting.

■ Prune grapes in the middle of winter to avoid excessive 'bleeding'.

■ Cover rhubarb plants in mid- to late winter to produce tender 'forced' shoots in early spring.

■ Check stored fruit and vegetables regularly and remove anything that shows signs of rotting.

■ Plant garlic in late autumn for bigger bulbs next year.

■ Harvest Jerusalem artichokes, endive, leeks and salad leaves.

■ Harvest brassicas (sprouting broccoli, cabbages, Brussels sprouts, cauliflowers and kale).

■ In late winter get an early start with vegetables like broad beans and Jerusalem artichokes. Chit potatoes.

■ Wash pots, seed trays and cloches.

■ Clean cold frames, polytunnels and greenhouses.

■ Projects for the winter: build a shed or paint and generally tidy up an existing one. Put in paths, make a compost bin and new raised beds and repair existing ones. Build a fruit cage or put up rabbit-proof fences.

A–Z of vegetables, herbs and fruit

Nowadays, there is an almost overwhelming choice of fruit and vegetables to grow in your allotment. They range from heritage varieties that have proved their value over many years, to newly introduced types developed for a range of reasons, such as to resist diseases or to crop earlier. Where to begin? Well, along with detailed growing information, each entry in this directory features a good selection of tried-and-tested varieties. This will get you going, but so much is a matter of trial and error. With each harvest you'll learn more about what you like and what does well on your plot.

Vegetables

The vegetables featured here are those that tend to do well in our climate, cropping reliably and being relatively trouble-free. They include very commonly grown types, such as potatoes, as well as more unusual ones, like Florence fennel. Along with your favourites, the trick is to grow a range of vegetables that will keep you supplied throughout summer and over the winter.

Artichokes, Globe

sow MAR, APR **plant** APR
harvest JUL, AUG, SEP

Globe artichokes are grown for their tasty flower buds, and they are very ornamental, too. They have silvery leaves that are cut like a thistle's and they reach up to 1.5m (5ft) tall. One or two plants are enough for the average family. They require a permanent bed on the allotment.

Cultivation
DIFFICULTY Easy; low input.
SOW under cover in early spring or in an outdoor seed bed in mid-spring.
PLANT out pot-raised seedlings in mid-spring. Also sold as young plants.
SPACE 90cm (3ft) apart.
CARE Provide a warm, sunny, sheltered spot in well-drained soil. In summer, water during dry spells when plants are carrying a crop. In mid-spring, feed each plant with slow-release fertilizer and mulch well. In autumn, cut down old stems as plants die down. Replace plants every four to five years; in year three, pot up some of the small offsets that form round their base to start a new row the following year.
HARVEST Allow them a year to establish before harvesting, and don't allow flowers to develop during the first summer – snip off buds as soon as you see them. Thereafter, from midsummer to early autumn, harvest half-grown (fist-sized) flower buds, using secateurs to snip through the stem about 2.5cm (1in) below the base of the bud.
STORAGE Artichokes will keep for a week in the salad drawer of the fridge.

Harvest artichoke flower buds in midsummer to early autumn, while they are still small and tender.

Look out for...
Blackfly can take hold; wipe them off developing buds with a damp cloth or a soft brush dipped in water. Earwigs can also be a problem. To remove them, soak the flower buds upside down in salted water before cooking.

Worth trying...
'Gros Camus de Bretagne' – French variety, hard to find as plants. Flavour is superb from very large heads.
'Gros Vert de Lâon' – Flavoursome French variety, widely available as plants.
'Violetto di Chioggia' – Available as seed or plants with pretty, mauve buds. Fair flavour but lightish crops.

Artichokes, Jerusalem

plant FEB, MAR
harvest OCT, NOV, DEC, JAN, FEB, MAR

Jerusalem artichokes are grown for their plump, knobbly tubers, which are baked, fried, roasted or stewed, just like potatoes. The plants are weather proof, even though the stems reach 3m (10ft) high, and low maintenance, so they make a particularly good allotment crop.

Cultivation
DIFFICULTY Very easy; low input.
PLANT egg-sized tubers 15cm (6in) deep in late winter or early spring. Save some of the best tubers from each crop to plant next year.
SPACE 40cm (16in) apart, with 90cm (3ft) between rows. Plant a double or triple row so these tall plants can support each other. This also makes a good windbreak.
CARE Use a general fertilizer when preparing the soil; no extra watering or feeding is needed. Flower buds can be removed to increase tuber yield, but in

Jerusalem artichokes give a good yield and can be harvested from mid-autumn through the winter.

practice this is unnecessary as the yields are high, and the sunflower-like flowers are a bonus. Stake plants in a windy site. You'll have a bigger crop if you earth up the plants when they've reached about 45cm (18in) high (*see* page 34).

HARVEST Dig them up from mid-autumn right through winter. When the plants start dying off in autumn, cut them back to 30cm (12in) high, after which you can simply dig up individual plants any time you want some tubers. Tubers still in the ground the following spring will start growing again, so use them before then.

STORAGE Leave them in the ground until they're wanted, as they store better there than anywhere else.

Look out for...
Generally trouble-free.

Worth trying...
'Fuseau' – Less knobbly tubers than normal, making them easier to clean and peel for cooking.

Asparagus

plant APR
harvest APR, MAY, JUN

Asparagus is pricey in the shops, to say nothing of being well travelled, so it's worth growing it yourself to enjoy it when it's really fresh. On the downside, it's a perennial and takes up plenty of space. You buy it as 'crowns' from specialist growers who have raised these for several years already. It still needs a further three years to settle in on your allotment before you get much of a harvest, but the plants may then continue cropping for 8 to 20 years.

Cultivation
DIFFICULTY Easy; medium input.
PLANT in well-drained ground or slightly raised beds on their own, adding plenty of organic matter the previous winter. Plant each crown in a generous hole,

spread the roots out then cover with 5cm (2in) of soil. Water well.
SPACE 30–45cm (12–18in) apart, with 60–90cm (2–3ft) between each row.
CARE As shoots start to appear above the ground, gradually earth up the plants until they are growing along ridges up to 15cm (6in) high (*see* page 34). In early to mid-spring, sprinkle general fertilizer over the asparagus beds; water if the weather is very dry during the cropping season. In autumn, cut the yellowed or browning ferns to 5cm (2in) above ground, then mulch the soil with well-rotted organic matter. Hand-weed beds often; don't use a fork for removing weeds, as the shallow roots of asparagus dislike disturbance.
HARVEST Do not cut any emerging spears for the first two summers after planting, and then take only a light crop in the first few weeks of the cutting season in year

There is little to beat the pleasure of eating your very own asparagus, freshly cut from the allotment.

three. From then on you can harvest as much as you like from mid-spring to early summer. Cut spears as soon as they reach about 15cm (6in) tall. Use a strong knife to cut them off 5cm (2in) below the soil surface and then refill the hole with soil to prevent pests from getting in.
STORAGE Don't store the spears – eat them as fresh as possible.

Look out for...
Self-sown asparagus seedlings grow quickly and are soon indistinguishable from those with pedigrees, except their output is generally much poorer. These interlopers will overcrowd beds, reducing the yield from your chosen variety.

Thin asparagus spears usually come from weak plants that have been cropped too early, cut too heavily in previous years, or not fed sufficiently – or all three.

Slugs also like emerging spears, and asparagus beetles eat the spears and foliage. The beetles appear from early summer and are yellow and black and about 1cm (½in) long; their caterpillar-like larvae are grey-black. Both beetles and their larvae can be picked off by hand, as can the clusters of black eggs on foliage. When cutting back the browning ferns in autumn, burn affected foliage to kill any pests that still may be lurking.

If you see blackfly while crops are growing, wipe them off developing buds with a damp cloth or a soft brush dipped in water.

Worth trying...
'Connover's Colossal' – An old favourite, readily available as both male and female plants – females are less prolific and shed seed, which can be a nuisance.
'Jersey Giant' – Long-season variety, cropping two weeks earlier than most and continuing to early summer.
'Jersey Knight' – Vigorous, heavy-cropping, all-male F1 hybrid, readily available from the mail-order firms. Thick spears and superb flavour.
'Stewart's Purple' – Sweet-tasting, colourful purple spears from mid-spring.

Aubergines

SOW FEB, MAR, APR plant JUN
harvest JUL, AUG, SEP

Aubergines need a long, warm growing season without much temperature variation, which means they're best grown in a greenhouse or polytunnel. If you want to try them outside on your allotment, plant them in containers or growing bags and position them in a warm, sheltered site. Keep them under cloches for as long as possible, then erect a windbreak around them. If you don't want to grow aubergines from seed, young plants are often available at garden centres or by mail order.

Cultivation

DIFFICULTY Not difficult, but need good weather for reasonable crops.
SOW at 21–24°C (70–75°F), in late winter or early spring. Prick out seedlings into small pots and grow on at 16–18°C (60–65°F) until mid-spring.
PLANT in a sheltered site in early summer. Harden off first and wait for warm weather.
SPACE 60cm (2ft) apart in all directions.
CARE Water sparingly at first, increasing the supply as plants start carrying a crop. Feed weekly with liquid tomato feed once the first fruits have set. Support with canes.
HARVEST from midsummer on, as soon as the fruits are 7.5cm (3in) long or more and while they are still shiny; use secateurs to cut the prickly stem 1cm (½in) beyond the fruit. Plants will continue to crop until cold nights strike in early autumn.
STORAGE Keep for a couple of weeks in the fridge.

Look out for…

Slow growth and low yields on poor plants are usually a sign that it is too cold, too wet or too windy. Greenfly can stop the plants growing, especially early on. Remove small infestations by hand or use a suitable spray. If red spider mite attacks the plants, pay more attention to watering, and spray water around and under the foliage too.

'Moneymaker' is a fine performer and suitable for outdoor cultivation, where it crops well in good summers.

Worth trying…

'**Baby Rosanna**' – Small plants – 60cm (2ft) tall – produce dark purple-black fruits that can be eaten when very small.
'**Moneymaker**' – One of the best outdoor aubergine varieties because the fruits mature quite early. Purple, sausage-shaped aubergines.

Beans, broad

SOW FEB, MAR, APR, NOV plant APR
harvest JUN, JUL

Broad beans are well worth growing if you have the space for a reasonable number of plants, and are prepared to provide sufficient support for them: home-grown and fresh from the allotment, they are far superior to any beans that you can buy, even those that are frozen within hours of picking. The flowers have a delicious fragrance, too.

Cultivation

DIFFICULTY Not difficult, but need regular care and attention.
SOW under cover in pots or trays in late winter and early spring, or outdoors *in situ* in early and mid-spring. Sow in succession in early and mid-spring and in late autumn for a longer season.
PLANT out indoor plants in mid-spring.
SPACE 20cm (8in) apart, in double rows 20cm (8in) apart, with 45cm (18in) between the double rows. If you have plenty of space, increase the double-row spacing to 60–90cm (2–3ft), which enables the plants to cope better with dry conditions and allows for easier weeding.
CARE Good support is vital. When the plants are still small, insert two 1.2m (4ft) posts side by side, about 30cm (12in) apart, at the ends of each double row of beans. Tie two horizontal strings between them along each side, at 30 and 60cm (12 and 24in) above the ground. It's vital to water the beans if the weather is dry.

Broad beans are a great, traditional allotment crop and worth growing for immediate use and for freezing.

HARVEST Once the beans inside the pods are the size of a thumbnail – over a six-week period from early summer – pick them by pulling back the pod against its direction of growth, then twisting slightly, or snip them with scissors or secateurs.

After cropping, if you don't need the space for something else, cut the plants down to about 15cm (6in) or so above the ground – you may get a late smattering of beans towards the very end of summer. STORAGE If you have any to spare, freeze them as soon as you pick them.

Look out for...

Mice and pigeons are fond of eating bean seeds; if this is a problem, start plants under cover. Cold, wet, early-spring weather can rot seed before it germinates; if your ground is poorly drained, cover the soil with tunnel cloches to dry and warm it before planting. Alternatively, sow seed a little later in the season.

The black bean aphid (blackfly) is a regular pest, congregating round the plant's tips and on young pods. Once pods start to appear, nip out the plant's growing-tips to remove their feeding sites.

Chocolate spot causes brown markings on the leaves. Prevent this fungus by feeding plants and providing good drainage and air circulation. Rust fungus produces red-brown markings on the leaves, but it occurs too late in the season to be a problem.

Pea and bean weevils chew notches in the leaves – although this looks unappealing, it seldom affects yields.

Worth trying...

'**Aquadulce**' – A tried-and-tested variety, particularly for early sowing. It can also be sown in late autumn for an early-spring crop in a reasonably mild winter.
'**Imperial Green Longpod**' – Bright green and tender beans in long pods on tall plants; a heavy cropper.
'**Medes**' – Short pods of tasty beans on mid-height plants. Sow only in spring.
'**The Sutton**' – Compact, 30cm (12in) tall, so needs less support.

Beans, French

Dwarf
SOW APR, MAY, JUN, JUL plant MAY
harvest JUN, JUL, AUG, SEP

Climbing
SOW APR, MAY, JUN plant MAY
harvest JUN, JUL, AUG

Flageolet, haricot
SOW APR, MAY, JUN plant MAY
harvest SEP, OCT

Green beans are near the top of the list of vegetables to grow. They don't take a lot of space or time and they are fantastic fresh – much better than those jet-setting imports that have seen more of the world than you have. If you become very keen, there is a wide range of types, including those that can be removed from the pod and dried, when they become either haricot or flageolet beans.

Cultivation

DIFFICULTY Not difficult, but need better conditions than runners; average input.
SOW in pots on a warm windowsill indoors in mid-spring; outdoors *in situ* in warm weather from late spring onwards.
PLANT pot-raised specimens after the

Beans for drying

To dry beans, leave the pods to grow to full size (once you do this, the plant will slow down production of new pods); they'll start to fade as the beans ripen. Let them dry out naturally, if possible. If damp or frost threatens, pick them and finish the drying in shallow trays in a warm, dry place indoors. Shell the pods, spread out the beans to dry further, then store in jars.

danger of frost is past; avoid planting if weather is cool, dull or damp.
SPACE Dwarf varieties 15cm (6in) apart with 25cm (10in) between rows; climbing varieties, including those for dried beans, on supports 20cm (8in) apart.
CARE Water sparingly while they are young and in dull, cool weather, more generously after they are established and carrying a crop.
HARVEST as soon as the pods are big enough. Pick regularly, or the beans get too fat and coarse. Dry out and save overgrown beans for next year's seed.
STORAGE Fine for a week in the fridge; can be frozen.

Look out for...

Cold, wet conditions may kill plants and will, at least, considerably reduce your yield. Sow and plant out slightly later to avoid problems.

Worth trying...

'**Blue Lake**' – Climbing variety with cylindrical green pods. Large pods can be left to dry out for haricots.
'**Cobra**' – Climbing, heavy and long cropper with slender, green pods.
'**Hunter**' – Climbing, heavy cropper with large, flat (like runners), very tender, tasty pods for slicing. Seeds can be difficult to obtain; '**Helda**' is similar.

Climbing French beans are succulent and tender, especially when eaten when small. Cropping is often prolific and the beans freeze reasonably well.

A healthy runner bean plant has a good supply of developing beans. Picking beans regularly ensures continued production.

'**Opera**' – Dwarf, reliable heavy cropper with excellent flavour. Disease-resistant, so good for organic growing.
'**Pea bean**' – Old variety with small pods of pea-sized, cream beans with maroon spots. These can be shelled and used fresh or allowed to dry in the pods on the plants. Can be difficult to find. Keep some pods for next year's seed.
'**Purple Teepee**' – Dwarf, heavy cropper with dark purple pods.
'**Soissons**' – Climbing bean with green seeds – flageolets when dry. Fine flavour.
'**Valdor**' – Dwarf, disease-resistant, heavy cropper; tasty pale gold pods.

Beans, runner

SOW APR, MAY plant JUN
harvest JUL, AUG, SEP, OCT

The secret with runners is to eat them while small and tender; beans that have been left to grow huge become tough and stringy. Don't feel guilty about chucking them on the compost heap, as chances are there will be plenty more young beans – these plants always produce bumper crops.

Cultivation

DIFFICULTY Easy; low input.
SOW in pots on a windowsill indoors in mid-spring, or outside *in situ* in late spring.
PLANT pot-grown plants in early summer.
SPACE 23cm (9in) apart in rows or grow them on wigwams.
CARE Provide tall supports – canes need to be 2.5m (8ft) tall, 30cm (12in) of which needs to be pushed into the ground. Water well in dry spells. Also, spray plants regularly, including open flowers. In very dry weather, soak plants thoroughly, then mulch them with garden compost or old newspapers. Never let the soil dry out. In

ground recently brought into cultivation, apply tomato feed weekly while cropping.
HARVEST as soon as they are upwards of 10cm (4in) long. When growing quickly, many large-podded varieties are still good at 30–38cm (12–15in). Once they have developed seeds they aren't worth eating.
STORAGE Put them in the fridge for up to a week if you must; can be frozen.

Look out for…
Birds may peck off the flowers and snails are partial to the pods and leaves. Flower drop may occur in dry weather.

Worth trying…
'**Borlotto Lingua di Fuoco**' – Red-dappled pods and maroon-and-white speckled beans; if the pods grow too big for using fresh, they can be dried like haricots (*see* box, opposite).
'**Enorma**' – Very long, straight pods; tender and tasty.
'**Lady Di**' – Long, slender, flavoursome, stringless beans; seedless until quite well developed, with a long growing season.
'**Sunset**' – Shortish beans with a good flavour early in the season.
'**White Swan**' – A heavy cropper with long, wide beans over a long period.

Beetroot

SOW MAR, APR, MAY, JUN
harvest JUN, JUL, AUG, SEP, OCT

Fresh beetroot is wonderful roasted or boiled, or even grated raw, and the tasty leaves can be used young in salads. When home-grown and picked while still small, beetroot is sweet and full of flavour – you'll never be able to face the pickled variety again. The natural, vivid purple colour of beetroot is caused by antioxidants, which, it is claimed, are good for your health.

Cultivation

DIFFICULTY Intermediate; average input.
SOW Early, bolt-resistant varieties in early spring; protect the rows with cloches, which may also give you an early crop of baby beets in a good year. Sow other varieties from mid-spring to early summer.

Beetroot have a long season: with successive sowing, you can start eating them in early summer and have the last ones in early winter.

SPACE Sow 'seed' 2.5cm (1in) apart in rows; thin seedlings to 7.5cm (3in) apart for babies, or 15cm (6in) apart for full-sized roots. (The 'seed' are capsules containing several seeds.)

CARE Water during dry spells to keep plants growing steadily. Weed to prevent young plants from being swamped. Protect plants with fleece in cold weather.

HARVEST as baby beetroot around 2.5cm (1in) in diameter. To thin, pull every third or fourth plant, leaving the rest with space to continue growing. Use full-sized roots as needed during summer.

STORAGE Roots tend to store best in the ground; lift the remainder in mid-autumn and keep under cover in a cool place to use as soon as possible. Can be kept in the fridge for up to two weeks.

Look out for...

Beetroot is very prone to bolting if sown too early or when growing conditions are difficult. Use varieties bred for early sowing if yours bolt regularly. Water more regularly if roots turn out woody.

Worth trying...

'Albina Vereduna' – White globes with a sweet flavour.

'Boltardy' – Bolt-resistant, traditional roots with a good taste and texture.

'Burpee's Golden' – Globe-shaped, golden roots; superb flavour. Good for picking small.

'Cylindra' – Tall, tubular roots form above ground, up to 20cm (8in) tall; produces a huge crop from a single row; no good for baby beet.

'Detroit 6-Rubidus' – Reliable, bolt-resistant globes for early crops. Doesn't get woody, even when large.

'Egyptian Turnip Rooted' – Excellent bolt-resistance; beetroot remains tender until the end of the season.

'Late Purple Sprouting' broccoli produces purple heads from early spring and has handsome leaves, too.

Broccoli, sprouting

SOW APR, MAY plant JUN, JUL
harvest JAN, FEB, MAR

Sprouting broccoli is incredibly tasty and a very reliable winter crop, not to be confused with the summer-cropping calabrese (*see* page 58). The sprouting spears are amazingly tender for plants that grow through winter, and this is one of those vegetables that is unbeatable picked and cooked within minutes.

Cultivation

DIFFICULTY Easy, low input.

SOW from mid-spring to late spring in a seed bed; thin to 7.5–10cm (3–4in) apart.

PLANT out young plants from the seed bed to the main bed in early to midsummer.

SPACE 45cm (18in) apart in each direction.

CARE Plant in very firm ground and water in dry spells. Give a general-purpose liquid feed in late summer, or a granular feed with lots of water. Support in windy sites.

HARVEST As soon as the colour of the developing heads is visible, cut the entire

Purple sprouting broccoli in summer

'Bordeaux' and 'Summer Purple' are summer croppers, although their season is brief. Sow seeds under cover at three-week intervals from late winter until early summer. Plant out seedlings from mid-spring and you'll have crops from midsummer. Combine these varieties with the winter ones and you could have tender shoots of sprouting broccoli all year round.

shoot 5–10cm (2–4in) long with a sharp knife. Check plants at least twice a week and don't allow shoots to run to seed; the more you cut, the more will grow; once they flower, they stop producing shoots.

STORAGE Keeps for up to three days in the fridge.

Look out for...

Most are amazingly pest-free, although summer croppers (*see* box, above) may be more prone to cabbage white butterflies; if the caterpillars strike, pick them off.

Clubroot can ruin crops and prevent you from growing brassicas for years. Pigeons can be a problem: cover brassicas with fine-mesh netting or bird netting.

Worth trying...

'Claret' – Very late – for picking in mid-spring; purple spears.

'Late Purple Sprouting' – Crops in early to mid-spring.

'Rudolph' – Very early, purple spears from early to late winter; large, tasty shoots.

'White Sprouting' – Crops in early spring; green-white spears.

Brussels sprouts

SOW FEB, MAR, APR plant MAY, JUN
harvest SEP, OCT, NOV, DEC, JAN, FEB, MAR

These slightly peppery mini-cabbages are fairly easy to grow and are far superior to the shop-bought sprouts. They are not to everyone's liking, but they are good for you: as well as being full of vitamins they contain antioxidants, which are thought to help fight cancer.

Cultivation

DIFFICULTY Easy; lowish input.

SOW at 13–16°C (55–60°F) indoors in late winter and early spring for early croppers, or in an outdoor seed bed in early spring and mid-spring for later ones.

PLANT out indoor-raised seedlings in late spring after careful hardening off. Those plants started off in seed beds can be transplanted in early summer. Make sure the soil is very firm; tread it down well before and after planting, using your heel around the plants.

SPACE 60cm (2ft) apart in all directions, further apart (75cm/30in) where there is more room.

The bubbly leaves of the Savoy cabbage 'Winter King' are perfect for combining with gravy and mashed potatoes.

CARE Water well in dry spells. Give a boost in the form of a general-purpose fertilizer in late summer and water in. Stake in exposed sites.

HARVEST as soon as they are large enough to eat – from the size of a large marble. Cropping from early varieties begins in early autumn, later ones from late autumn; the latest can be picked up until early spring.

STORAGE Keep for a few days in the fridge; can be frozen.

Look out for...

Pigeons can target the young plants, so use protection. Instead of forming tight buttons, sprouts sometimes 'blow' – they open out into small, flattened, green rosettes. Avoid growing them in loose soil and stake them. Clubroot is a threat.

Worth trying...

'**Darkmar**' – Heavy cropper with dark green sprouts from late autumn.
'**Falstaff**' – Mild, reddish-purple buttons from mid-autumn to early winter.
'**Trafalgar**' – Sweetish sprouts produced in heavy crops from early winter to early spring; tall plants.

Brussel sprouts are an excellent, long-lasting autumn and winter crop, and are sweet and delicious when small and freshly picked.

Cabbages

Spring-hearting
SOW JUL, AUG plant SEP, OCT
harvest APR, MAY

Summer- and autumn-hearting and red
SOW MAR, APR plant MAY, JUN
harvest AUG, SEP, OCT

Winter-hearting and Savoy
SOW APR, MAY plant JUN
harvest NOV, DEC, JAN, FEB

The name 'cabbage' encompasses a treasure trove of vegetables in a range of colours (white, green, red) and textures (smooth, crispy, deeply wrinkled). They are tasty, healthy and versatile. If you haven't yet tasted coleslaw made with your own home-grown cabbages, make this the year that you do. With careful planning, you should have cabbage varieties all year round.

Cultivation

DIFFICULTY Intermediate; it is worth a little extra care.

SOW under cover in early spring or in a seed bed from mid-spring onwards. Thin out and transplant as needed.

PLANT out summer and autumn cabbages, including red cabbage, in late spring and early summer; winter cabbage and Savoys in early summer; spring cabbage in early to mid-autumn.

SPACE Depends on the variety: allow 30cm (12in) apart for smaller ones; bigger ones need 45cm (18in). Increase spacing if you have more room.

CARE Keep watered in dry spells. Apply a top-up general-purpose or high-nitrogen feed during the summer to encourage leafy growth; water in well. Weed regularly, taking care not to disturb their shallow roots.

HARVEST when the centre tightens up and forms a solid 'heart'. Use secateurs or a knife with a scalloped blade to cut through the stem just below the heart. Remove damaged outer leaves. Retain the rest to protect the interior.

STORAGE Cabbages are best left attached to their stems in the ground until you want to eat them.

Look out for...

Cabbage white butterflies love brassicas, and their caterpillars eat the leaves and deposit frass (excrement), making them unfit to eat. Cover growing crops with fine-mesh netting and remove caterpillars by hand.

Small slugs can work their way into the hearts, making holes in them.

Pigeons like cabbages as winter forage: put bird netting in place if necessary.

Cabbage root fly lays its eggs at the base of the stem and the larvae eat the roots, causing the plant to wilt and die. Buy small crop-protection collars and slip these around the base of each stem to prevent egg-laying. Fine mesh properly fitted above and around the plants also helps. Clubroot can be a problem.

Worth trying...

'Cuor di Bue' (Bull's heart) – A full-flavoured winter cabbage with tight,

conical heads in late summer and autumn. The seeds can be hard to obtain.

'Golden Acre' – Summer-hearting, ball-headed cabbage; sow in late winter.

'Hispi' – Summer- and autumn-hearting; the one to choose if you grow no others. Tasty and fast-growing with small hearts. Sow from late winter under cover and from early spring to midsummer outdoors. 'Hispi' is also suitable as 'baby' veg: plant 23cm (9in) apart.

'January King' – Savoy cabbage tinged with red; matures in autumn and can be left in place throughout winter from a late-spring sowing.

'Kalibos' – Heirloom red variety with pointed heads.

'Red Jewel' – Good round-headed, red-leaved variety.

'Wheeler's Imperial' – Compact spring cabbage. Sow in summer for a spring harvest or late winter for an autumn crop.

'Winter King' – Savoy with crumpled leaves. Several sowings in late spring and early summer will stagger the crop, extending the season into late winter.

Calabrese
(green broccoli)

SOW MAR, APR, MAY plant APR, MAY, JUN
harvest JUN, JUL, AUG, SEP

Usually known as broccoli, calabrese is a really delicious and deservedly popular vegetable. It is similar to

sprouting broccoli (see page 56), but with solid, cauliflower-like heads. If you cut the central head and leave the plants in the ground, you get some smaller 'spears' a few weeks later – which makes it a good-value crop into the bargain. It prefers a sheltered spot and in colder areas may be best in a polytunnel.

Cultivation

DIFFICULTY Difficult; needs regular care.

SOW under cover in early spring, or in an outside seed bed from mid-spring.

PLANT pot-raised seedlings outdoors from mid-spring; transplant from seed beds in late spring to summer.

SPACE 30cm (12in) apart in each direction.

CARE Water and weed regularly and use a boost of general-purpose or high-nitrogen feed halfway through the growing season. Protect them from caterpillars by covering with a fine-mesh netting (make sure that the netting does not touch the leaves).

HARVEST from early summer into autumn. Cut off the whole head and use as needed.

STORAGE The heads will keep for a few days in the fridge if picked with a length of stalk.

Look out for...

They suffer the same problems as all the cabbage family (see left).

Worth trying...

'Crown and Sceptre' – A large central head in summer is followed by several pickings of smaller spears in late summer and autumn.

'Chevalier' – Medium-sized heads are followed by small spears from early autumn onwards.

'Kabuki' – Compact plants that mature early; grow closer together.

'Marathon' – A high-performance variety with dense blue-green heads.

Reliable in marginal conditions, calabrese 'Marathon' has medium-sized heads with an excellent flavour. Good for successional sowing.

Carrots

Early varieties
SOW MAR, JUL, AUG
harvest JUN, JUL, OCT, NOV

Carrots are fantastic eaten young, either raw or lightly steamed. When you grow your own you can enjoy experimenting with all the different coloured (and shaped) varieties, which are not available in the shops. Maincrop carrots (*see* box, below) are best for real carrot enthusiasts and those who want to eat organic, as organic carrots are expensive to buy.

Cultivation

DIFFICULTY Intermediate; pay attention and give regular care.
SOW thinly in shallow seed drills. Sow early varieties under cloches or fleece in early spring, then again in midsummer and late summer; cover these with fleece in autumn to extend the growing season.
SPACE Sow as thinly as you can. Allow 30cm (12in) between rows.
CARE Water well during dry spells and weed regularly. Take precautions against carrot fly; avoid thinning out seedlings, as the scent may draw carrot flies to your crop. Don't put carrots in ground that has been manured in the last 12 months.
HARVEST baby or salad carrots as soon as the first ones are big enough to use, leaving the rest to keep growing. Pull alternate carrots to give those left behind more room to grow.
STORAGE If necessary, store them in a paper sack in a cool place.

Maincrop carrots

If you want to grow maincrop carrot varieties, sow carrot seed *in situ* in mid- and late spring and early summer, when the soil has had a chance to warm up. You can leave the crop in the ground until rainy weather starts in autumn. After this, they are liable to produce fine, white root hairs and re-sprout, so dig them up, brush them off and let them dry. Washing them encourages rot.

The best carrots are those that are pulled when young and tender and eaten while they're still crunchy and full of flavour.

Look out for...

Carrot fly is almost inevitable. The best solution is to keep carrots covered with fine, insect-proof mesh. Grow rows of onions and spring onions around them to disguise the scent that attracts carrot flies. There are several carrot-fly-resistant varieties, such as 'Flyaway', 'Maestro' and 'Resistafly'. However, they are usually less tasty than other carrots and outbreaks of carrot fly may still occur.

There are nearly always one or two 'fanged' roots. If your whole crop is badly affected, you have probably added too much organic matter recently. Stony soil can produce the same effect though. With raised beds, this should not be a problem, but if your soil is rather coarse, try sieving it and mixing it with old potting compost.

Worth trying...

'**Autumn King**' – Large, tapering carrots; ready in autumn but will keep in well-drained ground over winter.
'**Healthmaster**' – Deep red-orange carrots with increased beta-carotene; use raw for the best nutritional benefits.
'**Nantes**' – Sweet-tasting, long roots ready in early summer from a protected late-winter sowing. 'Nantes' can also be sown at the same time as other earlies. Improved forms, such as 'Nantes 2', are identical.

'**Samurai**' – Red-skinned carrots with pink flesh that retains its colour even when cooked. Ready in summer and autumn.
'**Sugarsnax**' – Long, thin carrots for eating raw.
'**Yellowstone**' – Sweet, bright yellow carrots; best in salads.

Cauliflowers

Summer-heading cauliflowers
SOW JAN, FEB **plant** MAR, APR
harvest MAY, JUN, JUL

Autumn-heading cauliflowers
SOW MAR **plant** APR, MAY
harvest AUG, SEP, OCT, NOV

Winter-heading cauliflowers
SOW APR, MAY **plant** MAY, JUN
harvest FEB, MAR, APR

Cauliflowers have undergone a change: aside from the traditional white type, which we are all familiar with, you can now get green, yellow-green and purple, as well as mini-cauliflowers, which are one-per-person-size. However, for flavour and texture you can't beat the traditional white ones. On the downside, cauliflowers aren't a breeze to grow.

Cauliflowers are worth the extra trouble to grow well and they can provide crops almost all year round.

Cultivation

DIFFICULTY Advanced; look after well. Not time-consuming.

SOW summer varieties indoors at 16°C (60°F); autumn varieties indoors or in a seed bed under cover (such as a cold frame or under fleece outdoors) and winter varieties in a seed bed outdoors.

PLANT out healthy young plants when they are 7.5–10cm (3–4in) tall.

SPACE 60cm (2ft) apart for summer and autumn varieties; 75cm (30in) for winter varieties; 30–45cm (12–18in) for mini-cauliflowers.

CARE Keep plants well weeded and watered throughout summer. Boost the plants with a general-purpose fertilizer or high-nitrogen feed in mid- to late summer. As with all brassicas, firm soil is essential. Bend a few outer leaves over the cauliflower head as the curds bulk up. This is especially important for white varieties, which easily discolour.

HARVEST Once the developing curds form a dense, tightly packed hemisphere, cut off the head just beneath its base (include the collar of outer leaves as these will provide protection). Pick as soon as the head is level all over; don't delay.

STORAGE Wrap in clingfilm and store in a fridge for up to a week; can be frozen.

Look out for...

Cauliflowers suffer the same problems as cabbages (see page 58). Unfavourable weather can produce small or ruined heads, but inadequate soil preparation can also be a factor.

Worth trying...

'All Year Round' – Traditional white cauliflowers in autumn or spring. For spring crops, sow in mid-autumn and protect the plants under fleece.

'Autumn Giant' – Reliable autumn-header with firm, white curds.

'Avalanche' – Summer or autumn-header, good for both large heads and mini-cauliflowers. 'Igloo' is similar.

'Clapton' – An autumn-header with long leaves that protect the developing heads; resistant to clubroot.

'Purple Cape' – Purple heads in winter. Keeps its colour fairly well on cooking.

'Romanesco' – Lime-green curds form a series of pinnacles instead of a smooth, flat head; keeps its colour when cooked. Ready in late summer/autumn.

'Trevi' – Bright green and keeps its colour on cooking. Sow in spring, eat in autumn.

'Violet Queen' – Mauve heads ready in late summer/early autumn; turns green when cooked.

Celeriac

SOW MAR plant MAY, JUN
harvest SEP, OCT, NOV, DEC, JAN, FEB, MAR

With its lumpy, misshapen roots that grow half out of the ground, no one could call celeriac a very attractive vegetable, but it certainly is tasty, and it's much easier to grow than its refined relative, celery. It is one of those vegetables that are pricey in the shops, so it's worth your while trying to grow a few.

Cultivation

DIFFICULTY Intermediate; needs to be looked after well.

SOW in early spring on a warm windowsill or in a heated propagator at 16–21°C (60–70°F). Prick out and continue growing in warmth (13°C/55°F minimum). Keep well watered and in good light, but not strong sun.

PLANT in soil containing plenty of well-rotted organic matter after hardening off and when the last frost is safely past.

SPACE Minimum 30cm (12in) apart in all directions if you are restricted for space; 45cm (18in) apart if you can.

'Prinz' is a reliable celeriac variety with large, fleshy roots, perfect for soups and salads.

CARE Give general-purpose liquid feed every two weeks and keep plants well watered at all times. Weed regularly.
HARVEST from early autumn, as soon as the first roots are big enough. Dig up the whole plant, rest it on a hard surface and slice off the top, including all the leaves. Remove the smaller roots. You will need a strong, sharp knife. In mild winters you can have celeriac until early spring.
STORAGE Dig them up as you need them; they keep for a few days in the fridge.

Look out for…
Celery fly may cause problems, otherwise crop failure is usually due to cultivation deficiencies or adverse weather. However, imperfect roots are fine for making soups.

Worth trying…
'Monarch' – A reliable variety with good-quality roots.
'Prinz' – A tasty variety that is disease-resistant and may crop in late summer.

Celery
(self-blanching)

SOW MAR plant MAY, JUN
harvest AUG, SEP, OCT

Celery is delicious to eat raw and also imparts a wonderful rich flavour to a wide variety of stews, soups and other concoctions. However, it is very demanding and is one of the most difficult crops to grow successfully.

Cultivation
DIFFICULTY Advanced; challenging and time-consuming.
SOW in early spring on a warm windowsill or in a heated propagator at 16–21°C (60–70°F). Prick out seedlings into small pots as soon as they are large enough to handle, and continue growing in warmth

If you like a challenge, try growing celery. Success is hard to achieve, but the rewards are great.

(13°C/55°F minimum). Keep the plants well watered and in adequate light, but not strong sun. Harden off carefully.
PLANT out in rich, fertile soil that contains plenty of well-rotted organic matter, when the last frost is past.
SPACE 23cm (9in) apart in all directions. Close spacing ensures the plants shade each other's stems, which helps them to blanch. Grow them in blocks, with an edging of raised boards to prevent the stems of the plants at the edges being turned green by the light.
CARE Keep celery plants well watered; they must never go even slightly short of moisture. Give a liquid feed regularly from planting time onwards, using a general-purpose or high-nitrogen fertilizer. Keep well weeded until plants cover the ground sufficiently to shade out weeds for themselves.
HARVEST when the sticks are an edible size, in late summer. Self-blanching celery isn't hardy, so use it before the first frost.
STORAGE It will keep in a fridge for a few days but is better fresh.

Look out for…
Take strict precautions against slugs, starting several weeks before planting.

Celery fly can be a nuisance, mining the leaves and leaving blotches and ribbon-shaped tunnels. Pinch off and destroy any leaves that are affected. Carrot fly may also attack celery.

Worth trying…
'Victoria' – A self-blanching F1 hybrid; the easiest to grow successfully.

Chicory

SOW JUN, JUL
harvest OCT, NOV, DEC

Chicory is slightly bitter-tasting and forms heads rather like a lettuce, which can be cooked or used in salads. Witloof varieties are usually forced, which means they are grown without light to keep the leaves tightly furled, pale and tender. Other types, of which radicchio is one (it may be listed under 'R' in seed catalogues), are grown 'normally' for salad leaves.

Cultivation
DIFFICULTY Fairly easy; forcing varieties (see box, below) need time and effort.

Forcing chicory

'Witloof Zoom' is the standard forcing variety; others include 'Lightning' and 'Totem'. Grow the plants as usual and in late autumn cut down the tops to 7–8cm (3in) above the ground, dig up the roots and store them in buckets of slightly damp sand or soil in a cool shed.

Forcing takes three or four weeks. Depending on how much chicory you eat, force three or four roots at a time. Plant the roots in pots of moist compost, so their tops are just below the surface, then put in a warm, dark place. Check regularly and water lightly if necessary.

When the emerging buds are 7.5–10cm (3–4in) tall, cut them off at the base to use – don't wait, as they soon start to open and spoil. The same roots should produce several more 'chicons' before they need replacing with a new batch of roots from the shed.

SOW *in situ* – thin the seedlings, but don't transplant them.
SPACE 30cm (12in) apart in all directions.
CARE Water in dry spells and weed well.
HARVEST when they have formed hearts from mid-autumn onwards. Leave slowcoaches as they may heart up anytime until mid-spring. Forcing chicory should provide you with fare from midwinter.
STORAGE Remains fresh in the fridge for a week or two.

Look out for...
Red varieties can stay green. Red radicchio changes colour towards autumn. Green radicchio is edible if it has hearted up.

Slugs and snails are less of a problem than they are with lettuce.

Worth trying...
'Rossa di Verona' – Tightly packed leaves form mahogany-red radicchio hearts. Non-forcing.
'Sugar Loaf' – Upright, green-hearted non-forcing chicory with substantial inner leaves. Very reliable; good in polytunnels, where it can be left for some time in winter without rotting or bolting.

'Lightning' is one of several chicory varieties that are suitable for forcing.

Chillies

SOW FEB, MAR plant MAY, JUN
harvest JUL, AUG, SEP

Chillies come in a wide range of shapes, colours and 'heats': if you don't want your tongue set on fire, there are plenty of mild ones that add a pleasant zing to a meal. Start chillies off on a windowsill, then grow them on in a greenhouse or in a polytunnel if possible. Alternatively, plant them in a warm, sheltered site outdoors. Protect them with cloches for their first few weeks.

Cultivation
DIFFICULTY Relatively easy; low input.
SOW in pots or trays at 21–24°C (70–75°F).
PLANT in early spring by first pricking out the seedlings into 7.5cm (3in) pots. Move into larger pots if necessary, before planting out in a sheltered spot in late spring or early summer.
SPACE One or two plants of each variety should be plenty, but if you grow more allow 30cm (12in) between compact varieties, 45cm (18in) between the others and 60cm (2ft) between rows.
CARE Water sparingly, especially in cool conditions and while the plants are small. Feed weekly with liquid tomato feed. Provide support for the stems. In autumn pull up the plants and hang them upside down in a shed or not-too-hot kitchen to continue ripening, and let the chillies dry out naturally.
HARVEST Pick chillies as soon as they are large enough to use (when green, usually from midsummer), or leave them to reach full size and turn red and develop their full flavour. Snip off a whole chilli plus part of its short green stalk.
STORAGE Use fresh as required or dry them and store in clean, dry jars.

Look out for...
Greenfly may attack, especially early in the season. Wipe them off by hand or use an organic spray. A cold, dull or windy site or a poor summer can spell disaster.

'Hungarian Wax' produces long chillies that are relatively mild. It is a heavy cropper and easy to grow.

Worth trying...
'Hungarian Wax' ('Hungarian Hot Wax') – A reliable cropper with mid-strength yellow fruits ripening to orange then red.
'Jalapeño' – Short, mid-strength green/red chillies with a slightly cracked skin.
'Joe's Long Cayenne' – Long, slim chillies, ripening red with a fairly mild taste.
'Thai Dragon' – Large crops of slender, achingly hot, green then red fruits.

Courgettes, marrows and summer squashes

SOW APR plant MAY, JUN
harvest JUN, JUL, AUG, SEP, OCT

Once you've eaten a home-grown courgette you'll never want the thin-skinned, watery-flavoured, shop-sold ones again. Courgette plants are prolific – you'll need only one or two to have lots to eat. Marrows, which are more or less courgettes that have reached maturity, are good for stuffing and baking. Summer squashes, which come in a variety of shapes, can be grown and used just like courgettes.

Cultivation

DIFFICULTY Easy; low input.
SOW singly in small pots indoors from mid-spring.
PLANT out young plants in late spring or early summer, after the last frosts. Harden them off first.
SPACE 60cm (2ft) apart in each direction for the compact varieties, otherwise 90cm–1.2m (3–4ft) apart.
CARE Give them rich, fertile soil with plenty of organic matter; you can even grow them on the compost heap. Don't plant them out too soon, because they aren't hardy and you won't gain anything. They grow very rapidly once conditions are right. Water young plants carefully, increasing the quantity as they grow. Ideally, apply liquid tomato feed every week while plants are carrying a crop.
HARVEST as soon as they are big enough to use; courgettes from 10cm (4in), summer squashes from golf-ball size. Leave marrows until they are bigger (15–25cm/6–10in long). Cut through the stalk with a sharp knife. Avoid cutting into the plant or other fruits and discard any rotting, misshapen or damaged fruits. Plants will crop until mid-autumn.
STORAGE Best eaten fresh, but will keep in a fridge for up to a week.

Look out for…

Cucumber mosaic virus can affect plants, as yellow flecks at first, then the leaves turn increasingly yellow-patterned and crinkled and plants become stunted and unproductive. Choose resistant varieties where possible, and pull out and dispose of affected plants.

Powdery mildew often appears in the autumn. Improve vigour by liquid feeding and watering generously at the roots; remove the worst-affected leaves.

Young plants that fail to thrive are often found to have virtually no roots when dug up. This may be caused by harmful organisms in the manure or garden compost. To be on the safe side, start again with new plants in another spot. If fruits fail to develop it is almost always due to cool weather. Hand-pollination can help. The failure of female flowers to appear is usually also due to cold weather.

Worth trying…

'**Clarion**' – Pale green courgettes with a very mild flavour; good for using raw.
'**Defender**' – An early, heavy cropper producing dark green courgettes; resistant to the virus that can ruin courgette crops.
'**Orelia**' – Long, yellow courgettes on a vigorous plant.

'**Parthenon**' – A compact courgette with dark green fruits that set without needing to be pollinated.
'**Patty Pan**' – A summer squash with tasty, flying-saucer-shaped, pale green fruits.
'**Sunburst**' – Similar to 'Patty Pan' but with golden fruits.
'**Tiger Cross**' – A compact, virus-resistant variety, producing large crops of tender, light- and dark-green-striped true marrows (rather than overgrown courgettes).

Cucumbers

SOW APR, MAY **plant** MAY, JUN
harvest JUL, AUG, SEP

There is nothing quite like cutting your own fresh cucumbers and eating them while still standing out on the allotment. They are crunchy, tasty and very moreish. This book includes only the varieties that can be grown outdoors, but if you have a greenhouse or polytunnel on your allotment there are plenty of other kinds that you can grow.

Cultivation

DIFFICULTY Intermediate; need attention.
SOW seeds singly in small pots in mid- to late spring for outdoor plants.
PLANT outdoors from very late spring, after hardening off the seedlings. They need a warm, sunny, sheltered spot and are best trained on trellis or other supports, or grown over landscaping fabric to keep the fruits off the soil.
SPACE 45cm (18in) apart.
CARE Water sparingly at first and increase gradually as they come into full growth; when cropping, cucumbers need large amounts of water during hot weather. Feed regularly with general-purpose liquid fertilizer.

For good-sized fruits you should also prune the plants: on climbers, remove the lowest sideshoots up to 30cm (12in) above soil level; on all plants, remove the growing-tip when the plants have about seven leaves. This will encourage the

Courgettes are one of the most reliable and easy vegetable plants to grow. Just give them space and plenty of food and water.

'Burpless' is a reliable cucumber producing a good crop of thin-skinned, long, green fruit.

production of sideshoots. By the time each of these has grown about 15–20cm (6–8in) long, they should be carrying a tiny cucumber with a flower at the tip. Nip out the end of the shoot, one or two leaves beyond the developing fruit.

HARVEST The cucumbers are ready as soon as their shape fills out all the way along and they look big enough. You should eat them while they are still quite small. Don't wait for shop-sized fruits. Cylindrical cucumbers can be eaten at about 10cm (4in) long; rounded ones when they're 5cm (2in) long and wide.

STORAGE Best eaten fresh but will keep in a fridge for up to a week.

Look out for…

The plants are susceptible to powdery mildew, particularly at the end of the season, and cucumber mosaic virus. Choose disease-resistant varieties.

Bitter cucumbers are caused by variable weather conditions. Avoid problems by protecting the plants from extreme heat, dryness or cold.

Worth trying…

'**Burpless**' – Tender, crunchy, medium-sized fruits. This F1 hybrid is the best of all the outdoor varieties.

'**Crystal Lemon**' – Heavy-cropping variety with small, round, yellow fruits.

'**Long White**' – Mild-flavoured variety with short, cream-skinned fruits.

'**Marketmore**' – Cylindrical, dark green fruits on plants that can withstand poorish weather conditions.

Endive

SOW MAY, JUN, JUL
harvest SEP, OCT, NOV, DEC, JAN, FEB, MAR

Endive is like chicory in flavour and use but looks very different, with frizzy leaves in loose heads. If you like the bitter taste, it is a useful salad crop as it grows through the winter, making you less likely to have to trot down to the supermarket for a bag of sterilized green leaves.

Cultivation

DIFFICULTY Intermediate; get the details right and it's fine.

SOW *in situ* in rows 30cm (12in) apart from

Blanching endive

When endive plants are three months old, choose a few of the biggest plants to blanch. Blanching helps to reduce bitterness in the flavour of the leaves. Stand a heavy bucket or large clay flowerpot (with drainage hole blocked up) upside down over the top of the plant. Leave it in place for three weeks.

Alternatively, bunch up the outer leaves round the heart and use raffia or soft string to tie them in place – the result will be slightly less pale, but you will have fewer problems with worms or slugs. When one batch is ready, start to blanch a few more.

late spring; make successive sowings to have endive from early autumn to spring.

SPACE 30cm (12in) apart by carrying out gradual thinning.

CARE Water sparingly, increasing the supply slightly as plants mature. Plants remaining in the ground as winter approaches won't need watering. Protect endive that you intend to harvest through the winter. Cover them with cloches or fleece until you're ready to blanch them (*see box, above*).

HARVEST Cut the whole plant at the stem just above the ground. Trim off the tough outer leaves and use the soft, tender, yellowish leaves at the centre.

STORAGE Leave in the ground until the leaves are needed.

Look out for…

Slugs and snails like to hide inside blanching pots, where they snack on the heads of endive; remove slugs by hand and take anti-slug and snail precautions throughout the growing season.

Worth trying…

'**Moss Curled**' – Called 'frisée' in France; large heads of filigree foliage; tender and tasty when blanched. '**Kentucky**' is similar.

The crispy, curly-edged leaves of endive make a great addition to a green salad and have an unusual, slightly bitter taste.

Florence fennel

sow MAY plant JUN, JUL
harvest AUG, SEP

The swollen white bases of Florence fennel plants taste like aniseed and are delicious used raw in salads; they are even better cooked, particularly roasted with other vegetables in olive oil. Fennel needs a good summer to grow well, but it's worth trying if you want something unusual in your allotment. If you have a polytunnel, you have a greater chance of success.

Cultivation

DIFFICULTY Advanced; not time-consuming but demanding.
SOW Start plants off indoors in spring; sow three seeds each in small pots. Remove two and keep the strongest seedling.
PLANT Harden off seedlings carefully before planting them outside in a sunny, sheltered spot from early to midsummer; wait for a prolonged warm spell. You can sow and plant out a month earlier if you have a polytunnel.
SPACE 23–30cm (9–12in) apart each way.
CARE Water carefully – they need little water at first but must not dry out. As they grow and the weather warms up, increase watering and ensure the soil stays moist at all times. Feed with a general-purpose fertilizer. Cover outdoor-grown plants with fleece at night if it's chilly, even in summer.
HARVEST when they are the size of a tennis ball. Pull the whole plant up, trim off the root and lower leaves and cut the foliage back to a few centimetres above the top of the 'bulb'.
STORAGE Use as soon as possible after harvesting. Keep in the fridge for only a day or two.

Look out for…

Bolting, which makes fennel useless for eating, may be caused by dry soil, poor growing conditions, lack of organic matter or sudden swings in temperature. Also, slugs and other pests enjoy fennel.

Enjoy fennel bulbs when they're small and tender. They're not easy to grow but are well worth the effort.

Worth trying…

'Goal' – F1 hybrid, produces large bulbs with a good, aromatic fennel flavour.
'Victoria' – F1 hybrid with large, smooth, white bulbs. Resistant to bolting.

Garlic

plant FEB, MAR, NOV
harvest JUN, JUL, AUG

This little health-giving, breath-affecting bulb needs no introduction. It is an excellent addition to the allotment and good value in terms of time and output. If you grow onions, you can grow garlic. Don't plant garlic bought from the greengrocer's: choose properly prepared bulbs from a garden centre or seed catalogue.

Garlic is a rewarding crop and it's easy to grow enough bulbs to keep you supplied all year round.

Cultivation

DIFFICULTY Easy; low input.
PLANT whole cloves, ideally in late autumn but also in early spring. Autumn-planted garlic is ready earlier and usually makes larger bulbs, since it has a longer growing season. Choose the biggest cloves for planting and discard tiny ones. Push the cloves into the soil so the tip is about 2.5cm (1in) below the surface.
SPACE 15cm (6in) apart in each direction.
CARE Check occasionally and carefully replant any cloves the birds pull up. Water both autumn- and spring-planted garlic in dry spells in spring and summer.
HARVEST from early summer as 'wet' garlic – the plants are still leafy but there are reasonable-sized heads underground. Pull only what you need. Harvest the rest when the foliage starts to dry off naturally, in midsummer (autumn-planted) or late summer (spring-planted). When it has turned brown, dig up the plants and let them finish drying off on the ground in the sun. Try slicing up the stalks and using them as you would the cloves.
STORAGE Some varieties store well, others need using quite quickly. Dry them well after harvesting and store them in the house rather than a shed, where the cooler atmosphere may start them into growth. Use 'wet' garlic immediately.

Look out for…

Rust disease (red spots on the foliage) can kill the leaves prematurely, resulting in

smaller heads of garlic. It's often worse on ground that is poorly drained or rich in nitrogen fertilizer, but particularly where members of the onion family have been grown before, or debris from infected plants has been left behind or is in the compost. Destroy affected foliage, don't grow the onion family in that site for four or five years, and practise strict crop rotation (see page 27).

Bolting sometimes just happens. Don't worry about it: it doesn't affect the plant's ability to produce a good bulb.

Worth trying…

'**Lautrec Wight**' – Pink cloves with a white skin; stores until early spring.
'**Purple Modovan**' – Vintage, very pungent variety with mauve-tinged skin; use within four months.
'**Purple Wight**' – Early variety with purple-tinged cloves, ready for use 'wet' from early summer. Alternatively, store it until early winter.
'**Solent Wight**' – Bred for the British climate; ready from midsummer.

Kale

SOW APR, MAY, JUN plant MAY, JUN, JUL
harvest DEC, JAN, FEB, MAR, APR

Kale is the hardiest and most resilient member of the cabbage (brassica) family. It has its own characteristic flavour and softer leaves that wilt to be delicate and tender when they're steamed. If you're looking to eat vegetables in season, it's a must as it is harvested through the winter months, when few other fresh vegetables are available.

Cultivation

DIFFICULTY Easy; low input.
SOW in pots or seed trays out- or indoors.
PLANT Transplant into beds (with firm soil) as and when the seedlings are large enough to handle.
SPACE 45cm (18in) apart in each direction.
CARE Keep watered in dry spells through the summer.
HARVEST Pick a few leaves as soon as they are big enough, but don't take too many at once. Take your main harvest from a mid-spring sowing from early winter on. Leave the plants *in situ* over winter, as they enjoy a new spurt of growth in spring and produce a quick crop of succulent young leaves before running to seed.
STORAGE Keep leaves on the plant until they are needed.

Look out for…

Caterpillars can be a nuisance, but they are less of a problem with kale than on many other brassica crops. Remove them

'Pentland Brig' kale earns its place in the allotment, supplying leaves through winter, then delicious young shoots in spring.

by hand or use an organic pesticide; keep the plants covered with insect-proof mesh if caterpillars are a real problem. Clubroot is an ever-present threat.

Worth trying…

'**Black Tuscany**' ('Nero di Toscana') – Upright plants (can be spaced 30cm/12in apart); rich flavour from long and narrow, bobbly deep-green leaves. It can be picked from late summer through to early spring of the following year.
'**Pentland Brig**' – Tender, tasty, dual-purpose curly kale. Pick leaves in winter and the succulent shoots in spring; use the latter like broccoli spears.
'**Redbor**' – Bronze-purple curly kale with leaves that can be used young in salads.

Kohl rabi

SOW APR, MAY, JUN
harvest JUL, AUG, SEP

This odd-ball vegetable – a member of the cabbage family – tastes like a mild turnip when cooked, slightly sweeter raw. It's worth giving it a go as you'll rarely find it in the shops.

Cultivation

DIFFICULTY Intermediate; medium input.
SOW *in situ* from mid-spring.
SPACE Gradually thin out plants to 15cm (6in) apart in each direction.
CARE Provide well-prepared, fertile soil with plenty of rich organic matter. Keep well watered at all times.
HARVEST when the first globes reach golf-ball size (use these raw); eat them all before they reach tennis-ball size. Pull up whole plants, top-and-tail the globes and peel as thinly as you can.
STORAGE Keeps for up to two weeks in the fridge.

Look out for…

It can develop a woody texture, splitting or bolting due to poor growing conditions or lack of water. Clubroot could attack, but as the plant grows quickly it is rare.

The odd-looking, swollen stems of kohl rabi brighten up the vegetable garden as well as the dinner plate.

Worth trying…

'**Blue Delicacy**' – Late purple variety of kohl rabi with a mild, turnip-like flavour.
'**Kolibri**' – Purple globes with white flesh; a juicy F1 hybrid.
'**Logo**' – Fast-growing with white globes; slow to bolt.
'**Superschmelz**' – Green globes with white flesh; can grow huge, but is hard to find.

Leeks

SOW MAR, APR plant JUN
harvest SEP, OCT, NOV, DEC, JAN, FEB, MAR

Leeks are one of those vegetables that are perennially in vogue, and it's easy to see why. Tasty with a good texture, they are extremely versatile in cooking, have a long cropping season and are easy to grow. Choose two or three different varieties to have continuous supplies through autumn, winter and early spring, and grow summer baby leeks too.

Cultivation

DIFFICULTY Easy; little input.
SOW in seed beds in spring.
PLANT Transplant seedlings when they reach 15–20cm (6–8in) tall.
SPACE 15cm (6in) apart, in rows 30cm (12in) apart.
CARE Plant into fairly firm soil: make a hole 7.5–10cm (3–4in) deep for each seedling using a big dibber or a thick piece of cane. Drop each seedling in place without firming the soil around the roots. 'Puddle' them in with a watering can so the planting holes fill with water. Provide good growing conditions and plenty of water. Bolting can occur if plants aren't completely happy.
HARVEST a few at a time as soon as they reach a usable size: if you have plenty, pick them as babies and just top and tail them, otherwise wait until they are large enough to slice.
STORAGE Leave in the soil until needed; they keep in the fridge for up to a week.

Look out for…

Just like onions and garlic, leeks are prone to bolting. Use bolters instantly, even if they're still small, otherwise they'll be inedible. Leeks sown very early indoors (in midwinter) tend to produce more bolters than those sown outside in late spring.

Leeks also suffer from rust, as do all members of the onion family; salvage what you can by harvesting leeks to use early. Look out for rust-resistant varieties.

Baby leeks

'King Richard' gives a naturally early crop of long, slender leeks and is ideal for baby leeks. Prepare the ground well, as for a seed bed (*see* page 28). Sow thinly, making several sowings at three-weekly intervals from early spring to early summer. Thin the seedlings to 2.5cm (1in) apart, but don't transplant. Water carefully and give a regular feed with a general-purpose liquid feed. Start pulling baby leeks when they resemble spring onions. They'll crop from early summer until early autumn. If you have a polytunnel, a sowing in early spring will give you a late-spring crop.

Leeks are an easy crop to grow and can be left in the ground throughout the winter until you're ready to harvest them.

Worth trying…

'**Apollo**' – An F1 hybrid with good rust resistance; bred for winter use.
'**Bandit**' – An F1 hybrid producing long, sturdy stems that can be harvested until spring. Bolt- and rust-resistant.
'**King Richard**' – An early cropper (early autumn to early winter) (*see also* box, left).
'**Musselburgh**' – A reliable old variety that withstands hard winters; ready from early winter to early spring.
'**Neptune**' – This rust-resistant variety is also very hardy with long stems ready from mid- or late autumn.
'**Porbella**' – Good cropper over a long season from mid-autumn to late winter.

Lettuce and various salad leaves

Lettuce
SOW MAR, APR, MAY, JUN, JUL plant APR, MAY

harvest JUN, JUL, AUG, SEP, OCT

Salad leaves
SOW MAR, APR, MAY, JUN, JUL, AUG, SEP, OCT

harvest APR, MAY, JUN, JUL, AUG, SEP, OCT, NOV

Aside from the lettuces, there is a wide variety of other leafy plants that can be grown for use in salads (some are members of the cabbage family and so are suitable for cooking, too). You can grow the plants individually or as a mixed sowing for 'cut-and-come-again'; premixed seed packets are available. Most are easy to grow and can have a long cropping period from successional sowings (*see* page 32). If you have a greenhouse or polytunnel, you can extend the growing season.

Lettuces can be a challenge to grow well, but the easy conditions found in raised beds increase your chances.

Cultivation
DIFFICULTY Salad leaves are easy to grow well; lettuces need a bit more attention.
SOW Make early sowings of lettuces in pots or seed trays on a windowsill or in a propagator. Prick seedlings out into pots and transplant as the weather improves. Sow salad leaves direct and protect early and late sowings under cloches.
SPACE according to the variety: lettuces and other individual plants usually 25–30cm (10–12in) apart; cut-and-come-again varieties in rows 15cm (6in) apart.
CARE Lettuces and lettuce-based mixtures need plenty of water and rich, fertile, loose soil. The rest mostly like water but are less fussy about soil conditions, although brassica relatives, such as Chinese mustard greens, prefer firm soil.
HARVEST As you thin lettuces, eat any thinnings that are big enough; continue harvesting young plants to increase the spaces between those you want for full-size heads. Cut salad leaves as required as soon as they are large enough; cut stems near the crown of the plant to encourage new young growth.
STORAGE Pick and eat fresh; avoid storing.

Look out for...
Slugs and snails are a big threat to most salad leaves. Use a biological control from

'Lobjoits Green Cos' is the traditional cos with long, upright, crispy dark green leaves.

several weeks before sowing (*see* page 44). Flea beetles make pinprick holes in many salad leaves. Attacks rarely kill plants, but the damaged foliage looks uninviting. Cover plants with insect-proof mesh. If greenfly attack, brush them off.

With premixed salad leaf seeds, one variety is often stronger or faster-growing than others. When you spot the culprit, hoick some of it out while it is young to maintain a better balance of leaf types.

Bolting can occur in hot or dry conditions, particularly in poor soil; remove bolted plants to the compost heap, as the salad leaves will taste bitter.

Worth trying...
LETTUCES
'**Little Gem**' – A dwarf cos that is quick to mature with a good heart of crisp, tasty little leaves.
'**Lobjoits Green Cos**' – A crispy old-fashioned cos. Tie the leaves together to encourage the centre to heart.
'**Lollo Rossa**' – Worth growing for its red colour alone. Frizzy leaves and no heart.
'**Tom Thumb**' – A reliable small version of the round, butterhead lettuce.

OTHER SALAD LEAVES
Many salad leaves are sold as mixtures with names such as Mild Mix, Winter Mix or Spicy Oriental Mix. It's worth trying a range to find the one you like best.
Chinese mustard greens – Hot, spicy leaves that are suitable for cooking or eating raw in salads from June to October.
Mizuna – Good for salads. If used as 'cut-and-come-again', plants will provide leaves from June throughout the winter.
Pak choi – Crisp and crunchy, this is wonderful cooked as well as a great salad vegetable for June to October.
Rocket – The leaves add a lively piquancy to salads; they grow under almost any conditions from April to November.

Onions and shallots

Spring onions (spring/summer)
SOW MAR, APR, MAY, JUN, JUL
harvest JUN, JUL, AUG, SEP

Spring onions (overwintering)
SOW AUG, SEP, OCT
harvest FEB, MAR, APR, MAY, JUN

Bulb onions (maincrop, from sets)
plant MAR, APR
harvest AUG, SEP

Bulb onions (overwintering, from sets)
plant SEP, OCT
harvest MAY, JUN, JUL

Shallots (from sets)
plant FEB, MAR
harvest JUL, AUG

Onions are an easy crop to grow. Their close relatives shallots are even easier and have a lovely delicate flavour. Add spring onions to the mix, and you can enjoy an oniony taste in salads and cooking whenever you fancy it. If you have plenty of storage space, you can grow enough onions and shallots to keep you supplied for most of the year and you could even try pickling the shallots.

Cultivation

DIFFICULTY Easy; little input.
SOW a short row of spring onions every three or four weeks from early spring to midsummer, then sow an overwintering variety from late summer to mid-autumn. Sow thinly and thin out if necessary.
PLANT maincrop (summer) onion sets in early and mid-spring, and overwintering onion sets in autumn. Plant shallots in late winter and early spring.
SPACE Thin spring onions to 2.5cm (1in) apart, and allow 15cm (6in) between rows. Plant onion sets 10cm (4in) apart, in rows 20cm (8in) apart. Shallots produce offsets and need to be 20cm (8in) apart in rows 30cm (12in) apart.

'Red Baron' is a good all-rounder that is crunchy and sweet in salads, and is great for cooking, too.

CARE Keep plants watered in dry spells and weed regularly; take care as the roots are shallow. Keep the soil evenly moist.
HARVEST Use the thinnings of spring onions as you would chives, then pull alternate plants as baby spring onions; any left to grow can be used like mild onions. With maincrop onions, bend the tops over once the leaves start naturally turning yellow or brown; lift the bulbs of onions and shallots carefully when the leaves are completely brown and leave them in the sun to finish drying before storing in shallow trays in an airy shed. Use overwintering onions fresh from the ground from the time the first few reach usable size (around late spring).
STORAGE Pull spring onions for immediate use. Most maincrop onions and shallots keep well from early autumn until late winter. Store them in the light to avoid sprouting. Use overwintering onions within a month or so of harvesting.

Shallots produce many offsets from the original planted set so they need plenty of space to develop.

Seed or sets?

Spring onions are grown from seed, but shallots and onions are usually grown from 'sets'. These are small bulbs that have been raised from seed by commercial growers who then harvest them for sale. You can grow both onions and shallots from seed, but the seed is short-lived and must be sown fresh, so sets are a much easier option.

Look out for...

Bolting can be a problem in dry seasons. Choose a bolt-resistant variety and, where possible, buy heat-treated onion sets.

Mildew, a white or grey fungal growth, is disfiguring and debilitating. Cut off affected foliage and do not store bulbs.

White rot fungal disease affects onions and spring onions; it spreads rapidly and has no cure. The foliage turns yellow, then white cotton-wool-like stuff with black blobs in it develops near the base of the plant. The fungus remains in the soil so you won't be able to grow members of the onion family there for at least eight years, often more. Destroy affected plants and foliage and grow onions elsewhere. Practise crop rotation (see page 27) to minimize the risk of the disease recurring.

Worth trying...

'**Garnet**' – Maincrop (summer) onion, new version of 'Red Baron'; slightly earlier to mature.
'**Golden Gourmet**' – Shallot with large, tasty, golden bulbs. Good keeper.
'**Overwintering White Lisbon**' – Very hardy spring onion. Sow under fleece or cloches in autumn.

'**Prisma**' – Disease-resistant shallot with red skin and white flesh.
'**Radar**' – Gold-skinned overwintering onion; good for cold areas or bad weather.
'**Red Baron**' – Maincrop (summer) red onion with a fantastic flavour, mild enough for salads and also good for cooking; keeps well through winter.
'**Red Sun**' – Shallot with rounded bulbs. Red-brown skin. A long keeper.
'**Rosanna**' – Maincrop (summer) onion with pink flesh and red-brown skin.
'**Senshyu**' – Japanese overwintering onion with semi-flattened bulbs.
'**Sturon**' – Reliable, tasty maincrop (summer) onion; bolt-resistant; keeps well through winter.
'**White Lisbon**' – Classic, white-skinned spring onion for spring/summer sowing; grows on to produce white, silver-skin-type, golf-ball-sized onions.

Parsnips

Traditional parsnips
SOW MAR
harvest OCT, NOV, DEC

Baby-size parsnips
SOW MAR
harvest JUL, AUG, SEP

When you grow traditional parsnips, you have to be patient as they take about nine months to reach hearty roasting size, and they need space. But you can enjoy parsnips much sooner as babies, which take up less space. You will need proper baby-parsnip seed, as normal parsnip seedlings stay very thin until late in their life, so cannot be eaten early.

Cultivation
DIFFICULTY Intermediate; low input.
SOW thinly, about 2.5cm (1in) apart, *in situ* in deep, rich, fertile soil where manure was not used the previous winter; wait for mild weather if the soil is cold and wet.
SPACE Thin 'normal' parsnips to 15cm (6in) in several stages, babies to 5cm (2in).

'Avonresister' is a reliable traditional parsnip for roasting and hearty winter stews.

Space the rows 30cm (12in) apart; about half this for baby vegetables.
CARE Water in dry spells and weed often.
HARVEST from summer (babies) onwards. Dig up roots as required (after the foliage starts turning yellow).
STORAGE Leave them in the ground until needed unless it's very wet, in which case lift them and store in a frost-free shed.

Look out for…
Parsnips can be affected by canker. The roots develop brown scabs, especially round the top, which eat into the flesh. Less-damaged roots can be used once the canker is removed, but some are ruined. There is no cure; grow resistant varieties.

Plants may bolt, making the root fibrous and inedible, and roots may be 'fanged' (they are still edible). Both are down to poor growing conditions.

Worth trying…
'**Arrow**' and '**Dagger**' – Good baby types.
'**Avonresister**' – Canker-resistant and more resilient than most. Smallish roots, so space 7.5–10cm (3–4in) apart.
'**Tender and True**' – The one for flavour; long roots with small cores.

Peas

Early varieties
SOW FEB, MAR, APR, JUN, JUL plant APR
harvest JUN, JUL, SEP, OCT

Maincrop varieties
SOW APR, MAY, JUN, JUL
harvest JUL, AUG, SEP

Mangetout and sugar snaps
SOW APR, MAY, JUN
harvest JUN, JUL, AUG, SEP

If you want to grow peas, from a time, effort and result point of view it is best to stick to mangetout and sugar snap types, which are much better than the shop offerings – to say nothing of being less travelled. Shelling podded peas is fun, but it is difficult to do maincrop peas as well as the 'two hours from picked to frozen' brigade, who have the help of all sorts of high-tech equipment. Mangetout and sugar snaps are unaffected by maggots, which can ruin whole crops of 'normal' peas.

Cultivation
DIFFICULTY Intermediate; reasonable input.
SOW Sow seeds under cover in 5cm (2in) modules in late winter (this is easier if you have a greenhouse or polytunnel). Outdoors, sow in succession from early spring onwards. Make two or three staggered rows in a flat-bottomed drill about 20cm (8in) wide, so the seeds are about 7.5cm (3in) apart in each direction.
PLANT If you have raised early crops under cover, plant them out in staggered rows, with plants 10–15cm (4–6in) apart in each direction.

SPACE 45cm (18in) between sets of rows for short varieties; 90cm (3ft) for tall ones.

CARE Provide plant support. After sowing, push pea sticks in along the rows of short-growing varieties. Tall varieties are best with 2m (6ft) posts and horizontal wires holding up pea netting. Water plants in dry weather and weed regularly.

HARVEST when they reach a usable size. Mangetout pods are best at 5cm (2in) long; they never get fat but they can get stringy, so pick and discard any that have 'gone beyond it'. Sugar snaps are best at about 4cm (1½in) long but can be shelled if they've grown too large. Check the progress of shelling peas by popping open one or two of the biggest pods – use them while they're still young, tender and sweet.

STORAGE Eat fresh or freeze peas as soon as you pick them.

Look out for…

Seeds may be eaten by mice or other rodents, and can succumb in cold, wet soil at sowing time.

Powdery mildew on young leaves and tips of shoots can spread to cover whole plants. The disease is worst on dry soil and old plants. Keep plants well watered and ensure good air circulation.

Pea weevil makes irregular notches in the margins of leaves; all but the most badly infested young seedlings nearly always grow out of it without problems.

Maggot larvae of the pea moth tunnel into the pods of shelling peas to eat the seeds and deposit their mess. They can ruin a whole crop of plants. Crops sown early or late in the season seem to be less affected. You can also cover plants with insect mesh. Mangetout and sugar snap peas don't seem to be susceptible.

Foot-and-root rot kills the roots – they turn black and the young plants turn yellow. It may be due to overwatering poorly established small plants in cold, dull weather, or an organism in the soil. Put new seeds or plants in a different area of ground and practise crop rotation (*see* page 27).

Peas are really delicious raw. You're more likely to pick and eat them immediately than bring them home for cooking!

Worth trying…

'**Alderman**' – Traditional, 2m- (6ft-) tall shelling variety; late to start cropping, but productive over a much longer cropping season than dwarf pea plants.

'**Feltham First**' – Round-seeded shelling pea suitable for the very earliest sowings. These dwarf plants, 45cm (18in) tall, need little support.

'**Golden Sweet**' – Tall mangetout (2m/6ft) with decorative mauve flowers, pale green leaves, red leaf nodes and yellow pods.

'**Hurst Green Shaft**' – A delicious maincrop variety, 75cm (30in) tall. Long and heavy cropping.

'**Kelvedon Wonder**' – Wrinkle-seeded shelling variety, with good flavour, on dwarf plants 45cm (18in) tall.

'**Oregon Sugar Pod**' – Tall mangetout reaching 1m (40in) high, with a fairly long cropping season.

'**Sugar Ann**' – Tall sugar snap variety, 1.5m (5ft) high; needs support but crops for a reasonable length of time.

'**Sugar Snap**' – Early sugar snap variety on dwarf plants 75cm (30cm) tall.

Peppers

SOW FEB, MAR plant MAY, JUN harvest JUN, JUL, AUG, SEP

Home-grown peppers are like a more concentrated version of the ones you can buy in the supermarket; they are perhaps less thick-fleshed and juicy, and are usually smaller, but far more flavoursome. It's easy to get the green fruit, but ripening to red is more likely on plants grown in a polytunnel or greenhouse rather than outdoors.

Cultivation

DIFFICULTY Easy; little input.

SOW on a windowsill indoors or in a heated propagator at 21–27°C (70–80°F). Prick out the seedlings into individual small pots when large enough to handle, and grow on at 16–19°C (60–65°F).

PLANT from very late spring to mid-summer. Harden off before planting out.

SPACE 45cm (18in) apart, individually in pots or two to a growing bag.

CARE Water in after planting, then water sparingly until plants are growing strongly

Green peppers straight from the plant are crunchy and have a tangy flavour, quite unlike that of the shop-bought ones.

and starting to flower or bear fruit. Feed weekly with liquid tomato fertilizer after the first flower opens to encourage plenty of fruit. Tie the main stem to a cane.

HARVEST Use secateurs to pick green fruits when big enough to use. Peppers are unlikely to ripen on outdoor plants, except in a long, warm summer. Leaving fruits to ripen discourages the production of more peppers.

STORAGE Peppers stay fresh for a week or so in the fridge.

Look out for...

Greenfly affect peppers, so check plants regularly and wipe off greenfly with damp tissue, or use an organic insect spray.

Plants can fail to produce fruit if growing conditions are poor (lack of sun, cold, dull or windy weather); overwatering can also cause crop failure. In a poor summer, try to move them under cover for shelter, or drape them with fleece at night and on cold or windy days.

Worth trying...

'Bell Boy' – Heavy cropping and reliable. The fruits start green, ripening to red. There are other 'Bells' in various colours.
'Big Banana' – Long, tapering peppers to 25cm (10in). Green, ripening through yellow to red.
'Matador' – Bull-horn-shaped sweet peppers; red when ripe.
'Redskin' – Compact, bushy plants with oblong green peppers, ripening to red.

Potatoes

First earlies
chit FEB, MAR plant MAR, APR
harvest MAY, JUN, JUL

Second earlies
chit FEB, MAR plant APR
harvest JUN, JUL, AUG, SEP

Maincrop
plant APR
harvest SEP, OCT, NOV

Today, a huge range of potato varieties is available to gardeners: bakers, chippers, mashers, salad spuds, novelty and coloured ones, and heirloom varieties – as well as a selection of disease-resistant kinds.

Spuds are not grown from seed, nor from any sprouted leftovers you have in your vegetable rack. Instead, you must buy 'seed' potatoes in late winter or early spring. These are tubers grown especially for the job and are certified disease-free.

Potatoes are known as first earlies (new potatoes), second earlies and maincrop, depending on when they are ready for harvesting.

Cultivation

DIFFICULTY Easy; little input.
PLANT first earlies in early to mid-spring; second earlies a week later and maincrop potatoes a week after that. Plant all tubers 13cm (5in) deep.
SPACE first earlies 30cm (12in) apart in rows 60cm (24in) apart; second earlies and maincrops 40cm (16in) apart in rows 75cm (30in) apart.
CARE Hoe between rows to keep down weeds until the potato shoots are 15cm

(6in) high, then earth up the plants (see page 34). If frost threatens, earth up as soon as the shoots appear above ground. Except in a long, dry summer, you shouldn't need to water potatoes.
HARVEST From early summer (first earlies), midsummer (second earlies) and autumn (maincrops). Use a fork carefully to loosen the soil around each individual plant. Take a handful of stems at the base and gently pull – the potatoes will come up with the roots. Sift through the soil for the rest.

Earlies often produce enough fair-sized tubers for a meal even before the plants start to flower (flowering is a good indication that the crop is ready). Use your fingers to pull a few out without disturbing the plants, which will continue to grow.

Maincrops keep quite well in the soil even after the haulm (foliage) has died down, but need lifting before the weather turns wet to prevent attack by black keeled slugs. They may also start to grow again, which affects their keeping qualities.
STORAGE First and second earlies are fine in a cool place for a week or so. Store maincrops, dry and with the soil brushed off, in brown paper or hessian sacks in a cool, dark place.

Look out for...

Potatoes are popular with keeled slugs, which are more common in very humus-rich soil. Avoid problems by planting them in ground that has not had compost or manure added for about a year (this also suits the crop-rotation plan suggested on page 27) and use a biological control (see page 44). If you need to add compost to improve very poor soil, do this no later than the previous autumn, so it has a chance to rot down before planting. Also, there are varieties that resist slug damage.

Always grow a few new potatoes on your allotment. 'International Kidney' ('Jersey Royal') is about the best known, with a wonderful taste and texture.

Chitting potatoes

It is traditional to 'chit' first and second early varieties in late winter or early spring to get them started into growth, before planting them out when the weather warms up. This gives them a head start as their growing season is shortish. You don't need to chit maincrop spuds, as they have a much longer growing season.

Chitting involves sitting the tubers in a box, such as an old egg box or seed tray, with the growing end facing upwards – recognizable by the cluster of tiny buds ('eyes') on it. Keep them in good light but out of direct sunlight. When the shoots are 1–2.5cm (½–1in) long, the potatoes are ready for planting.

Tubers affected by scab (irregular corky patches on the skin) look unattractive but are still edible if peeled. Scab is more prevalent on light soil that dries out badly in summer, especially on chalky ground, so you may need to add organic matter, but make sure you do this at least a season before planting.

Potato blight is the most serious potato disease. Outbreaks are most likely in a wet summer; affected plants develop brown patches on the leaves (in damp conditions you'll also see white fungal rings around the spots) in late summer and the foliage quickly yellows and dies. Early potatoes are rarely affected, as the tubers have usually been lifted before blight strikes, but if midsummer is rainy, start spraying plants with Bordeaux mixture to prevent the disease. Once it gets hold there's no cure. Dig up affected crops straight away and destroy the remains (do not compost).

Several different viruses affect potatoes: the edges of the leaves roll inwards, or leaves may develop yellow mosaic patterns. Viruses are often spread by aphids, but also occur when people save their own tubers to replant instead of buying seed potatoes. Affected plants are stunted with low yields.

Worth trying...

FIRST EARLIES

'**Duke of York**' – Pale yellow tubers for new potatoes or to grow on as later maincrop potatoes; a good choice if you have room for only one variety.
'**Foremost**' – Firm, waxy, white, salad new potato. Eat hot or cold.
'**Mimi**' – Small, pink-flushed tubers with compact foliage.
'**Pentland Javelin**' – Delicious white, waxy salad potato; disease-resistant.
'**Rocket**' – Fast-growing early; large crops of round white tubers; disease-resistant.

SECOND EARLIES

'**Charlotte**' – An attractive and highly popular, superb salad potato with golden skin and firm, waxy, cream-coloured flesh.
'**Edzell Blue**' – Purplish skin gives this tasty Victorian variety its name. The very floury white flesh makes it a great masher.
'**Estima**' – Large, oval, yellow-fleshed tubers, excellent as summer bakers; plants do well even in dry summers.
'**International Kidney**' – Kidney-shaped tubers with a waxy texture.
'**Kestrel**' – Off-white tubers with purple rims around eyes. A good all-purpose variety; fair disease resistance.

MAINCROP

'**Golden Wonder**' – A late maincrop with red-brown skin and a superb flavour that improves with age. Best for baking, roasting and frying.
'**King Edward**' – Old favourite with red-variegated tubers, known for its superb flavour, with cream-coloured flesh. Good for roasting and baking, but needs good growing conditions to do well.
'**Mayan Gold**' – Long, slender golden tubers with firm, golden, nutty-flavoured flesh. Great deep-fried whole or roasted; breaks up when boiled.
'**Picasso**' – White-skinned potato decorated with splashes of pink. Cream-coloured tasty flesh. Good for all uses.
'**Pink Fir Apple**' – This variety makes the most fabulous potato salad and is also great baked, if you like a crispy skin. A very late maincrop with long, slim, knobbly tubers, best left in the ground until late autumn. Stores well right through winter.

Radishes

Summer radish
SOW MAR, APR, MAY, JUN, JUL, AUG
harvest MAY, JUN, JUL, AUG, SEP

Winter radish (including Chinese, Japanese, Mooli)
SOW JUL
harvest AUG, SEP, OCT, NOV

Radishes are the traditional accompaniment to a typical English salad, but can do so much more besides in stir fries and as crudités.

'French Breakfast' is probably the best-known and most widely grown radish. Its mild flavour makes it ideal for summer salads and crudités.

They are a very quick crop, and need continuously good conditions to be tender and juicy and to avoid bolting. There are also oriental and winter radishes with large roots ready to pull in autumn and winter – they are worth trying for a change.

Cultivation

DIFFICULTY Intermediate; average input to provide what they need.

SOW *in situ* in succession throughout the growing season.

SPACE Thin summer radish seedlings to 2.5cm (1in) apart; allow 15cm (6in) between rows. Thin winter radishes to 5–7.5cm (2–3in) apart with 30cm (12in) between rows.

CARE Ensure soil is rich and well drained, but avoid ground that's recently had organic matter dug in or roots may split or 'fang'. Keep plants watered and well weeded. Thin out seedlings early.

HARVEST as soon as the first summer radish reaches usable size. Don't delay – they grow fast and then turn tough and woody, or bolt. For winter radish, harvest from late summer on. You'll have to dig, not pull, them up.

STORAGE Summer radishes are best eaten straight away, but will keep for a few days in the fridge. Winter ones should be dug up by late autumn and can be stored for a short time in a dry, frost-free shed. Mooli varieties keep quite well until midwinter.

Look out for...

Poor soil, hot or dry conditions can all cause bolting.

Overcrowding or leaving it too late before thinning out seedlings will prevent roots developing freely.

Flea beetles can attack (*see* lettuce, page 68); in severe cases they may kill small seedlings.

Worth trying...

'**French Breakfast**' – Traditional, cylindrical summer radish; red with a small white area at the base; very reliable.
'**Mantanghong**' or '**Beauty Heart**' –

Chinese winter radish; huge, tennis-ball-sized with green rind over red flesh. Crisp and sweet; makes good 'vegetable crisps' or crudités.
'**Mirabeau**' – Long, thin radishes with the traditional pink-and-white colouring.
Mooli – Various types of Japanese winter radish with often huge, hot-tasting, long, tapering to cylindrical white roots.
'**Scarlet Globe**' – Traditional, round, red summer radish.

Spinach

Summer spinach
SOW MAR, APR, MAY
harvest APR, MAY, JUN, JUL

Autumn spinach
SOW AUG, SEP, OCT
harvest SEP, OCT, NOV

Spinach is so convenient to buy in neat bags, ready washed, but it is also fairly easy to grow and you can have it much cheaper and fresher that way, bursting with health-giving nutrients. Most of the modern varieties are dual-purpose: you can eat them raw in salads, when the leaves are tiny, or cooked when they're bigger.

Cultivation

DIFFICULTY Intermediate; low input.

SOW thinly in rows *in situ*. If you want baby salad leaves, sow every four to six weeks during the sowing season.

SPACE by thinning to 2.5cm (1in) apart for baby leaves, or 7.5cm (3in) for cooking-size leaves – use thinnings in salads.

CARE Provide well-dug, nitrogen-rich, fertile soil. Water and weed well. It's essential for the plants to grow steadily without a check. Seeds sown in early summer are less likely to succeed as it is too hot and dry for most spinach varieties.

HARVEST baby leaves as soon as they are big enough to use, usually within a month of sowing. Cut the crop little and often. For cooking, start cutting leaves when the plants reach a suitable size (six to eight weeks after sowing) – don't wait too long or they will bolt.

STORAGE Best eaten when they have just been picked, but will keep for a couple of days in the fridge and can be frozen.

Look out for...

Bolting is triggered by high temperatures, shortage of water or poor soil with insufficient organic matter. Sow frequently for a continuous supply. Downy mildew can also affect crops; disease-resistant varieties fend off all but the worst attacks.

Worth trying...

'**Bordeaux**' – Bright red leaf-stalks and leaf-veins make this ideal for baby salad leaves. Can also be sown in late winter and from late summer to autumn.
'**Galaxy**' – Mildew-resistant variety for baby leaves. Can be grown through winter under cover, even on a bright windowsill.
'**Medania**' – All-round variety for sowing in spring or summer to produce 'baby' spinach leaves, also in autumn to grow under cover for cutting in spring.

The red-flushed leaves of 'Bordeaux' spinach add colour to a green salad and look good on the allotment, too.

Spinach, perpetual

SOW APR, MAY, JUN, JUL
harvest JUL, AUG, SEP, OCT

Perpetual spinach is excellent for providing a green, leafy vegetable nearly all year round, and you're unlikely to find it in the shops, so it's well worth growing on the allotment. It is less fragile than 'real' spinach; the same plants are easily capable of surviving the hotter summer months and on through winter in milder areas. Its leaves are a bit milder than proper spinach – more like Swiss chard in taste and texture, but without the thick midribs. Only one variety is usually available.

Cultivation

DIFFICULTY Easy; little input.
SOW thinly in rows *in situ*.
SPACE seedlings by thinning to 15cm (6in) apart with 30cm (12in) between rows.
CARE Keep plants watered in dry spells and weed regularly.
HARVEST as soon as the leaves are big enough to use; don't over-pick plants; cut little and often from all over the row and allow plants to recover between times.

Winter crops

Sow a row of perpetual spinach in midsummer under a cloche or in a greenhouse or polytunnel border. The resulting plants will stay in perfect condition all winter and start growing again in spring, producing enormous crops of large, tender, unblemished leaves until they run to seed in late spring.

Alternatively, sow perpetual spinach seed outdoors in midsummer and protect the plants with fleece over winter (*see* pages 37–8). They can survive the cold without protection, but the leaves will be battered and unfit to use.

STORAGE Best eaten just-picked, but will keep for a couple of days in the fridge.

Look out for...

Slugs can be a nuisance, but this is really a trouble-free crop.

Perpetual spinach is an easy crop with a long season and it requires remarkably little care – just pick and eat.

Squashes and pumpkins

SOW APR plant MAY, JUN
harvest AUG, SEP, OCT

Squashes and pumpkins make huge plants and need plenty of room – and they don't repay the space with quantity, it must be admitted. However, they are easy to grow and kids love them. Pumpkins are good for soup and for making Halloween lanterns, while squashes tend to be more versatile and are great roasted or in stews. (For summer squashes, *see* pages 62–3.)

Cultivation

DIFFICULTY Easy; low input.
SOW singly in pots on a windowsill indoors or in a heated propagator at

Pumpkins can reach a prodigious size and are often the focus of keen competition among allotment-holders.

18–24°C (65–75°F). Grow on at 13–18°C (55–65°F) – a cool room or shaded, sheltered cold frame is ideal.

PLANT Harden off and plant when the last frosts are past.

SPACE 90cm (3ft) apart.

CARE Plant in very rich, well-manured soil or dig a large pit in autumn and spend winter filling it with materials you'd usually put on the compost heap. In spring, cover it with a mound of soil and plant there. You can even grow them on the compost heap – put a few inches of soil on top first. After planting, surround each plant with a ring of soil, about 30cm (12in) from the stem; fill this 'saucer' each time you water.

Water sparingly at first. As the plants get going, water regularly and apply liquid fertilizer. Weed until the plants cover the ground. Slowly reduce feeding and watering in late summer, and in early autumn remove foliage over-shadowing the fruits so the sun can ripen them.

HARVEST Tiny pumpkins can be eaten like courgettes. Leave some to grow to full size and ripen on the vine. For storage, cut them with a short length of stem. Raise them all up off the ground by mid-autumn to prevent them from rotting.

Monster pumpkins

To grow a monster pumpkin, first choose the right pumpkin variety, such as 'Big Max', 'Atlantic Giant', 'Hundredweight', 'Dill's Giant Atlantic' or 'Sumo Giant'.

Start plants and harden off as normal. Plant using the pit and compost method (*see above*). After planting, cover the plant with a cloche or fleece for protection (uncover it on fine days), until it grows too big or the weather really warms up.

Allow three fruits to set and start to swell, then select the largest and remove all the rest. This means the plant directs its energies into just the one fruit. Weed, water and feed as normal. You could bury the trailing stems in very good soil, only just covering them. They will grow roots to help feed your pumpkin. For greater chance of success, grow several plants, spaced 2–3m (6–10ft) apart.

STORAGE Allow the fruits to dry in the sun, turning them over. Store them in a dry, frost-free shed or garage where they should keep for several months, or bring them indoors to a dry, coolish room.

Look out for...

Mosaic virus can cause problems – look out for yellow mottling on the leaves and poor growth. Destroy affected plants.

Mice and larger rodents may nibble the skins of pumpkins. Slugs may damage young fruits while the skins are very soft, and damaged areas deform as the fruits grow larger, although this doesn't affect taste. However, deep wounds may allow in fungal organisms, which cause rot.

Worth trying...

'Avalon' and **'Harrier'** – versions of the butternut squash sold by greengrocers. The true butternut is unlikely to ripen even in a good summer, but these have been bred for our weather conditions.

'Becky' – The ideal Halloween pumpkin.

'Crown Prince' – Medium-sized, squat, steely blue-grey pumpkins with orange flesh; good for roasting and pumpkin soup.

'Hasta La Pasta' – Long, bright orange, marrow-like squash; it yields 'vegetable spaghetti', obtained by baking whole then removing the shredded flesh using a fork.

'Sweet Dumpling' – Small, green-striped, cream squashes produced at the rate of four to six per plant. Delicious baked and stuffed whole or sliced and roasted.

Swedes and turnips

Swedes
SOW MAY, JUN
harvest SEP, OCT, NOV, DEC, JAN, FEB

Turnips
SOW APR, MAY, JUN, JUL
harvest JUN, JUL, AUG, SEP

Swedes and turnips are easy to grow and can be eaten when they are still very small. When young and tender, turnips are good to eat raw, while

Swedes are a good crop for harvesting over a long season, lasting well in the ground until heavy frosts are forecast.

swedes are excellent mashed; they are traditionally eaten with haggis on Burns' Night. Both are very tasty when roasted, to say nothing of adding bulk, texture and flavour to stews and soups. Because they keep their shape well when cooked, they are also good cut into cubes and put into pies; swede is an important ingredient in Cornish pasties.

Cultivation

DIFFICULTY Easy; little input.

SOW seeds thinly *in situ*. Turnips from mid-spring, swedes a few weeks later, from late spring or early summer.

SPACE seedlings by thinning in stages. Swedes should be thinned to 23cm (9in) apart with 40cm (16in) between rows. For baby turnips, thin to 2.5cm (1in) apart, otherwise allow 10–12cm (4–5in) between plants; leave 23cm (9in) between rows.

CARE Plant in an open, airy situation in full sun. Hoe regularly. Keep the soil evenly moist, as wide fluctuations between wet and dry conditions can cause the roots to split or become fibrous and tough.

HARVEST Turnips are best small, 5cm (2in) across at most. Any larger and they can be woody. Swedes can be bigger, but you don't have to wait until they're the size of the ones in the shops. Harvest as you want them; leave the rest to keep growing.
STORAGE Swedes keep best in the ground until needed, but dig them up if your garden is on heavy clay or if prolonged freezing temperatures are forecast. Turnips will keep for a few days in the fridge.

Look out for…
Like all brassicas, both turnips and swedes can suffer from clubroot. Choose a resistant swede variety; there are currently no resistant turnips. Powdery mildew can also be a problem in swedes; there are a few resistant varieties.

Turnip gall weevil may invade turnip roots, causing distortion similar to clubroot. Cut the root open: the weevil will have made a tunnel. Throw away affected roots.

Flea beetles make small holes in turnip leaves, so use fine mesh for protection.

Worth trying…
SWEDES
'**Brora**' – A new variety with excellent flavour, purple skin and yellow flesh.
'**Invitation**' – Modern variety with purple-flushed skin, bred for resistance to clubroot and mildew.
'**Marian**' – The traditional flavoursome variety with purple tops and yellow-cream bases; resistant to mildew and clubroot.

TURNIPS
'**Atlantic**' – Reliable turnip, like a flattened ball with a purple top. Known to the French as 'navets'.
'**Golden Ball**' – A round turnip with flavoursome golden flesh.
'**Snowball**' – Long-established turnip with sweet, white flesh.

Sweetcorn

SOW APR **plant** MAY, JUN
harvest JUL, AUG, SEP

For true fans, the only way to eat sweetcorn is picked fresh from your own crop and cooked minutes later. The sugars start to turn to starch as soon as the cob is removed from its parent, so every minute counts. If you find frozen or tinned sweetcorn too sweet it could be that you are eating the supersweet varieties; try growing a 'normal' variety – you may find it more to your taste.

Cultivation
DIFFICULTY Easy to intermediate; lowish input.
SOW one seed per small pot on a windowsill or in a heated propagator at 16–21°C (60–70°F) in spring. Grow on in slightly cooler temperatures. Harden off for planting out when the frosts are over.
PLANT sweetcorn in blocks, not rows; the plants are wind-pollinated and this is the best way of ensuring good pollination.

'Golden Bantam' sweetcorn is a reliable heirloom variety that produces tender, sweet kernels.

Plant them slightly deeper than the soil level in the pot. This encourages tillering (putting out small sideshoots and more roots) and makes the plants more stable.
SPACE 45cm (18in) apart in each direction.
CARE Cover young plants with fleece on cold nights to help them establish quickly. Water in dry spells. No support is needed, even though the plants grow quite tall.
HARVEST as soon as the cobs ripen in late summer. You can tell they are ripe as the silky tassels turn brown and dry up, but you should double-check by testing the cobs, too: peel back a little of the leaf-like green sheath to expose a few kernels and press a thumbnail into one or two – if clear liquid spurts out the cob is not quite ripe; when it's ready the juice is milky.
STORAGE Eat or freeze as soon as picked.

Look out for…
Poor pollination can mean that you have gappy cobs – areas without kernels. They are still edible.

Best eaten when small and tender, turnips are reputedly very good for you. The leaves are edible, too.

Fruit fly larvae distort the developing tips of young plants so that they grow stunted and twisted and produce unusable, underdeveloped cobs. Protect young plants with insect-proof mesh and pull out and destroy affected plants.

Worth trying...

'**Applause**' – Supersweet F1 variety.
'**Golden Bantam**' – An old favourite, producing long cobs early in the season.
'**Incredible**' – Sugar-enhanced, reliable variety; ripens mid-season.
'**Minipop**' – Baby corn cobs 10–15cm (4–6in) long; plant 20cm (8in) apart and pick while the tassels are still silky and pale.
'**Sundance**' – 'Normal' F1 variety with 18cm (7in) cobs; matures early and crops reliably, even in poor summers.

Swiss chard

SOW APR, MAY, JUN, JUL
harvest JUL, AUG, SEP, OCT

Swiss chard is a great, green, leafy vegetable, like a mild spinach but with more substance – it doesn't cook down to mush. The leaves can be steamed or cooked like spinach; the leaf-stalks boiled like celery. As well as being tasty, it looks attractive on the allotment, with its big, shiny foliage and white, orange or red leaf-stalks and leaf-veins.

Cultivation

DIFFICULTY Easy; very little input.
SOW in rows in mid-spring to midsummer.
SPACE 15cm (6in) apart with 30cm (12in) between rows.
CARE Keep plants watered in dry spells and weed regularly.
HARVEST as soon as individual chard leaves are big enough to use, around midsummer from early sowings. Use a sharp knife to cut through each stalk at the base of the plant. Early-sown chard plants are usually finished by autumn, but midsummer-sown crops often withstand a mild winter. If there's a really cold spell they may die down, but they will regrow in spring to produce a short-lived crop of tender leaves before running to seed in late spring.
STORAGE Pick and use fresh.

Look out for...

Snails can make a meal of them, but they often prefer to hide in the bigger leaves, which you won't want to eat anyway. Otherwise, this is a trouble-free crop.

Worth trying ...

'**Bright Lights**' – A mixture of red-, white- and yellow-stemmed varieties; its decorative qualities are its main asset. The thinnings can be used to brighten salads.
Ruby chard – Slender, bright red stems and purple-tinged dark green leaves; it is not quite such a strong grower as Swiss chard, so grow it if you want decoration as well as food.

Easy to grow as well as attractive on the allotment, Swiss chard tastes like mild spinach and keeps its texture better when cooked.

Tomatoes

SOW MAR plant MAY, JUN
harvest AUG, SEP

Cherry, plum and giant beefsteak, yellow, brown, white and striped – you could eat a different tomato almost every day of the year, so great and wide is the choice. They are not the most accommodating of plants, though, being quite demanding and prone to almost as many problems as there are varieties, but even if you experience difficulties one year, you're sure to succeed the next. In the end, home-grown tomatoes are worth it. If you have a greenhouse or polytunnel on your allotment, you'll be able to enjoy crops about a month earlier and a month later. Take care when choosing tomatoes to grow outdoors, as not all are suitable. All those mentioned here are fine both indoors and out.

Cultivation

DIFFICULTY Bush tomatoes are easy; cordon tomatoes are trickier.
SOW seeds on a windowsill indoors or

Supporting and training tomatoes

Cordon (single-stemmed varieties) need a single cane, while bush varieties do better with three shorter canes to support their bushier shape. Tie the main stems to the cane or canes to stop them being weighed down by the developing crop and breaking. Tie in new growth every week.

With cordon tomatoes, every week remove all the sideshoots that grow in the angle where each leaf joins the main stem. Bush tomatoes don't need their sideshoots removed; if they grow too big and bushy, thin out the growth.

In late summer, start removing new flowers (they'll never fruit) and remove the growing-tip (or tips, in the case of bush varieties). Remove a few of the lower leaves, especially those that are already yellowing, to allow more light and air to circulate.

in a heated propagator at 18–21°C (65–70°F) in early spring. You can sow a little bit later if you live in a cold area.
PLANT after the last frost is safely past, in a warm, sheltered spot in the ground or in growing bags.
SPACE 75cm (30in) apart with 90cm (3ft) between rows.
CARE Start feeding with liquid tomato feed while the young plants are still in their pots, prior to planting out. After planting, feed once a week, or twice a week once they start carrying a crop.

Immediately after planting, give each plant ½ litre (1 pint) of water, then – weather depending – let it go slightly short of water until the first flowers open. Gradually increase watering when the green fruits start to swell; every few days is fine for plants in the open ground, but those in growing bags will need more frequent watering.

Support the plants well and tie up and trim them regularly (*see* box, opposite).
HARVEST straight from the plants when they have ripened fully, usually from late summer. If you aren't going to eat them straight away, break them off just above the green calyx to help them keep better. In a good season, fruit will continue to ripen well into autumn.

When you want to clear the plants, remove any full-sized green tomatoes and keep them in a dark place indoors. Don't put them on a sunny windowsill – this makes them shrivel up without ripening. Instead, put them in a box with a ripe apple or banana, both of which give off ethylene gas, which hastens maturity.
STORAGE Eat fresh, or make into sauces to freeze and enjoy later in the year. Alternatively, make chutneys and relishes.

Look out for...
Tomatoes are susceptible to potato blight (*see* pages 44 and 73). Keep a close watch for early symptoms (brown patches on the leaves), particularly if there is rain in early and midsummer and, as with potatoes, spray outdoor tomatoes with Bordeaux mixture as a precaution. Repeat every

fortnight and you may save the crop. Once leaves start looking dead and both ripe and unripe fruit develop brown, rotten-looking patches, it's too late. A few blight-resistant varieties are available.

Split fruit occurs as result of stress, caused when plants are alternately wet and dry at the roots. Avoid it by watering little and often. Pick affected fruits – they're usually the riper ones anyway – and purée them so they don't go to waste.

Blossom end rot is a sunken, black, leathery patch on the base of the tomato. It is most common in fruit in growing bags and is caused by the plants drying out. To prevent it, water regularly.

Botrytis might occur in damp seasons and where plants are overcrowded. It affects different parts of tomato plants in different ways: fluffy, grey, sunken patches on stems; grey, mouldy flowers that drop off without setting fruit; small, round, translucent 'ghost spots' on the skin of green tomatoes. Avoid growing plants too close together. Remove lower leaves to increase air circulation. Remove all affected parts as soon as you notice the problem.

Whitefly are rarely a problem outdoors. They live on the undersides of the leaves

If you want plum tomatoes, 'Roma' is a good choice, with heavy crops of dense-fleshed fruit.

and fly out when you tap the plant. They suck sap and secrete sticky honeydew, which may then grow sooty mould. If you had an attack last year, grow companion plants (*see* page 46). Under cover, sticky traps can be effective, but they can also catch beneficial insects.

Worth trying...
'Ailsa Craig' – Cordon variety with round, red fruits.
'Gardener's Delight' – Hugely popular cordon; big trusses of sweet, cherry-sized tomatoes over a long period.
'Ildi' – Cordon bearing masses of small, sweet, yellow plum tomatoes.
'Marmande' – Beefsteak cordon with lobed, red fruits; 'stop' the plants (remove the tops of the main stems) after two or three flower trusses have set fruit, as they can't support a huge crop.
'Roma' – Bushy variety reaching waist-high; flavoursome, juicy, red plum fruits.
'Sungold' – Cordon with lots of small orange-yellow, sweet-tasting fruits.
'Tornado' – Bush variety that does well even in a poor summer, with very well-flavoured, round, red fruits.

'Gardener's Delight' always scores highly for taste and texture and it is a good cropper, too.

Herbs are very much part of the fruit and vegetable garden and your allotment won't feel complete without them. Easy to grow and nearly always trouble-free, they make the perfect accompaniment to many of the dishes you'll prepare with your home-grown produce. A great number are also long-lived and flower for several months, so as well as adding to the appearance of your allotment, they are invaluable for attracting insects for pollination and pest control.

Many herbs do very well in reasonably fertile soil with plenty of water and good drainage and will grow happily with your vegetables. However, some prefer dry, gritty, low-nutrient soil, so set aside an area for those that thrive in poor conditions (*see* box, below).

Basil

Basil has a strong, clove-like aroma and taste that goes very well with tomato dishes. It is fairly easy to grow from seed, although it does take a while to reach a good size for harvesting.

Sow the seed in pots on a windowsill indoors – every few weeks in late

Preferred soils

BEST GROWN IN FERTILE SOIL	BEST GROWN IN POOR SOIL
Basil	Marjoram and oregano*
Chives*	
Coriander*	Rosemary*
Dill	Thyme*
Fennel	
Mint*	*Flowers popular with bees
Parsley	
Sage*	

spring and early summer to ensure a continuous supply. Thin the resulting seedlings, but leave several in each pot for a bushy 'plant'. Keep the plants in pots, or plant them out about 15cm (6in) apart in well-drained, humus-rich soil. Nip off the top of each stem to encourage branching and more leaves. Remove flowerheads when they appear; basil is an annual and will die after flowering.

Bay

An ingredient of bouquet garni and a wonderful, aromatic addition to a wide variety of stews and savoury dishes, bay is a shrubby tree that can grow to 12m (40ft) in warm regions. However, it is easy to keep smaller with pruning. Plant it in a permanent, free-draining site in late spring or early summer. Once it starts producing new growth, pick a few leaves whenever you need them for cooking.

Chives

Chives are related to onions and have long, thin, hollow leaves with a mild oniony flavour. They are an excellent addition to salads, particularly potato salad. Rounded heads of lavender-purple flowers appear in early summer and attract bees.

Plant chives in fertile, well-drained soil and give them plenty of water during dry periods. Dig up, divide and replant the clumps at any time to increase your stock.

Make annual sowings of short-lived herbs in order to have a continuous supply.
① The most popular basil, 'Genovese'.
② Dill becomes a tall, feathery plant.
③ Curly-leaved parsley, 'Moss Curled'.

Coriander

The seeds of this tall, aromatic annual herb are used in the Indian spice garam masala. Both the leaves and the seeds are also wonderful in soups, salads and many other dishes.

Sow the seeds in a warm, sunny, sheltered spot with good drainage from late spring to midsummer. Harvest the leaves little and often, leaving a short length of stalk, 2.5–5cm (1–2in) long, to resprout. If you want leaves only, buy varieties such as 'Cilantro' and 'Leisure', which are bred specifically for foliage production. Allow one or two plants to go to seed to use in cooking or to grow for next year's crop.

Dill and fennel

These two herbs are similar in taste and appearance. Their aniseed-flavoured, feathery leaves are ideal with fish; the seeds are also used in cooking. Fennel has slightly finer, greener leaves than those of dill, which are blue-green, and there is a purple-leaved fennel, too. Both are easy to grow, but dill really needs warm, dry weather. Dill is shorter, at up to 90cm (3ft) tall, while fennel can reach 1.8m (6ft).

Sow seeds very thinly in pots from mid-spring to early summer. Plant the seedlings in clumps in a well-drained, sunny position; thin carefully as necessary. Have separate plants for leaf and seed harvesting, because removing leaves will affect seed production. Dill is an annual, so keep some seed for next year's plants. Fennel is perennial; cut the stems down in autumn and they'll resprout next year. Remove the seedheads to ensure you don't get masses of self-sown seedlings.

Marjoram and oregano

Marjoram and oregano have a similar flavour and are used in pizza toppings, Greek salad and lamb dishes. They're easy to grow from seed, germinated in pots on a windowsill indoors in mid-spring. Plant out the seedlings in clumps without thinning, 23cm (9in) apart, in poor to moderately fertile soil in a hot, dry spot. Grow pot marjoram (*Origanum onites*), an evergreen perennial, and sweet marjoram (*Origanum majorana*), an annual, for the best flavours.

Mint

There are many different varieties of mint and they are cheap to buy as small plants; *Mentha spicata* is the one most commonly used for mint sauce with roast lamb and added to new potatoes and peas during cooking. Most culinary mints need plenty of moisture and reasonably fertile soil. Where happy, they spread widely, so prevent this by putting them into bottomless pots, which you then plant into the ground.

Parsley

Curly-leaved parsley needs no introduction and its close relative Italian or French parsley, which has flat leaves, is equally useful in the kitchen. Sow seeds *in situ* or in pots to plant out. It is important to keep root disturbance to a minimum, so thin very carefully to about 15cm (6in) apart. Parsley likes deep, richly fertile, moist

soil and can cope with some shade. Germination can be slow, usually due to cold conditions, so sow a row or two about every three months in order to ensure continuous supplies. The plants are biennial but are usually best replaced annually.

Rosemary

Great with everything from roast potatoes to lamb and in salad dressings, rosemary leaves have a sharp but heady aroma. The evergreen, shrubby plants do best in poor to moderately fertile soil in a sheltered, sunny area, but will often survive in less-than-perfect conditions, including quite shady spots. Allow the plants to establish and begin growing steadily before harvesting.

Sage

The soft-textured leaves of sage are known for their use in stuffings, but also make wonderful additions to sauces and breads. Sage makes a large, billowing bush, which can be cut back hard in spring. It is best in light soil in a sunny spot, but it can grow in a wide range of well-drained conditions. Wait until the plant has established and is growing strongly before harvesting.

Thyme

Thyme has tiny, aromatic leaves that can be added to breads, stuffings, stews and risottos as well as being an ingredient of bouquet garni. The

It's worth having a good selection of long-lived herbs.
① Bay
② Sage
③ Pineapple mint
④ Marjoram

low-growing plants need poor, neutral to alkaline soil with very good drainage and a bright, sunny spot. They do well in pots. Although thyme is hardy, it won't survive winter where conditions are less than ideal, but it is inexpensive to buy as young plants each spring. *Thymus vulgaris* is considered best for cooking, but you can experiment with other varieties: there are plenty.

Other herbs to try

Chervil – Low-growing biennial that has carrot-like leaves with a delicate aniseed flavour; good for adding to buttery sauces, omelettes and chicken dishes.

French tarragon – Perennial with aromatic leaves; good with meat, fish and vegetable dishes.

Lemon grass – Perennial with sharp-edged, grassy leaves that are used in Thai cooking; needs a warm spot.

Lovage – Tall, perennial herb with celery-like leaves but much easier to grow.

Savory – There are two types: winter and summer savory; the leaves of both are good with vegetables and pulses.

Fruit

Allotments are great places to grow a range of smaller fruit plants as well as one or two trees if you have space. You'll need to plant them well (*see* page 31) and prune them properly (*see* pages 39–42), but otherwise they almost look after themselves. This directory includes the more commonly grown allotment fruit plus one or two more unusual types you might like to try.

Apples

harvest JUL, AUG, SEP, OCT, NOV, DEC

Apples are remarkably easy to grow. On an allotment, where space can be tight, it's generally best to plant small freestanding trees, cordons and stepovers on dwarfing or semi-dwarfing rootstocks (*see* box, below right); their small size also makes pruning and harvesting easier. Avoid larger apple trees. Some apples need a pollinating partner to produce fruit (*see* box, opposite).

Cultivation
DIFFICULTY Easy but need pruning.
PLANT in a sheltered site with fertile, deep, well-drained soil. Most trees on dwarfing rootstocks must be supported by a stake throughout their life. They also need a 90cm- (3ft-) diameter circle of weed-free, bare soil around them.
SPACE cordons 45cm (18in) apart, stepovers 2m (6ft) or more apart.
CARE Water in after planting. Dwarf rootstock trees need watering thoroughly in dry spells when they are carrying fruit. Well-established trees on semi-dwarfing rootstocks should not need watering, except in periods of prolonged drought.

Mulch every spring while the soil is moist. Feed with general-purpose fertilizer from mid- to late April.
HARVEST as soon as they start ripening – early varieties are ready from late July to September. These early varieties don't keep, so use them straight away. Lift the fruit in your hand and gently twist; if it parts easily from the tree, it's ripe. Leave later varieties on the tree until mid-October, unless high winds are forecast.

Famous for its wonderful fruit, 'Bramley's Seedling' is very widely grown and is *the* cooking apple.

STORAGE Store apples in a dryish place that has a constant cool temperature, such as an airy shed or garage. Place them in single layers in shallow, stackable trays that air can circulate around, or put them in large, loose plastic bags with air holes punched in them. Clean, dry fruit in perfect condition should keep until Christmas, but check them regularly and remove any that are starting to go bad before the rot spreads. Alternatively, cook and freeze any surplus.

Pruning
Once established, freestanding apple trees need attention only to remove damaged wood as well as light pruning in winter to encourage fruit production. Supported trees, such as cordons, fans and espaliers need more regular pruning (*see* page 40).

Apples have two types of fruiting habit: spur-bearing and tip-bearing. The two types are pruned slightly differently (*see* box, page 40).

Look out for...
Maggots in ripe apples are normally codling moth larvae. These tunnel through the developing core and are easy to cut out. Hang up codling moth traps from mid-May to mid-August – these are non-chemical pheromone traps (*see* page 31) that lure the males to a sticky pad, which prevents the females being fertilized. Pheromone traps work better if neighbours with apple trees use them too.

Scab produces brown or green spots on the foliage, blistered shoots and scabby, distorted fruit. Spray as directed with a suitable fungicide, rake up fallen leaves and prune out badly affected shoots – burn both. Resistant varieties are available.

Nectria canker cracks the bark, which shrinks back in flakes, usually in concentric rings. Badly affected branches may die off. Some varieties are resistant. Prune out badly affected shoots or even whole branches. Copper-based fungicide helps control it – spray twice in autumn. Bacterial canker is similar.

Fireblight is a bacterial disease that blackens flowers, leaves and shoots, which wilt as if they had been burned. Oozing cankers may be found on infected stems at blossom time. There is no cure; remove affected branches, taking a good margin of healthy growth,

Rootstocks
Fruit trees are almost always grown on rootstocks. These ensure particular characteristics, such as restricted height, fruiting at a young age and vigour. Choose dwarfing or semi-dwarfing rootstocks (M27, M9 and M26 in apples), because these will produce short trees that are easy to look after and harvest.

Apples can be bought as stepovers, which are tiny trees only 30cm (12in) high, grafted onto very dwarf rootstocks. They are ideal for edging paths and produce normal-sized fruit.

too. Disinfect your pruning tools and destroy the prunings.

Bitter pit occurs in stored apples (they develop small brown surface spots that may spread through the whole fruit) and is probably caused by calcium deficiency and water shortage during growth. Mulch the trees and water well in summer.

Worth trying…

'**Braeburn**' – Crunchy, tangy, red-and-yellow fruit. Self-fertile; harvest mid-October until just after Christmas.
'**Bramley's Seedling**' – The most popular cooking apple, with large, green fruit; crops well in alternate years. Mid-season flowers; needs two pollinating partners, but pollination rarely seems a problem. Ready from August, picked fruit keeps well from November to March.
'**Discovery**' – Bright red, small to medium-sized eating apple with crisp flesh when fresh. Early flowers; harvest from late August to late September.
'**Egremont Russet**' – Rough-skinned, pink-flushed, light brown eating apple. Distinctively flavoured, crisp flesh. Early flowers; harvest in October. Will keep but best eaten immediately.

'**Fiesta**' – A crunchy, red eating apple with a zingy flavour. Mid-season flowers; harvest October to November.
'**Greensleeves**' – Medium-sized, green-yellow eating apple, crisp with a sharp flavour. Mid-season flowers; harvest September to November.
'**James Grieve**' – Cooking and eating apple with sherbet-flavoured, medium to large, pale yellow fruit streaked with red. Self-fertile. Pick green for cooking from mid-August; leave to ripen for eating from September.
'**Idared**' – Cooking and eating apple with red fruit that keeps well. Early flowers; harvest from late October.
'**Sunset**' – Eating apple that can replace 'Cox's Orange Pippin' (which is prone to disease and poor cropping). Mid-season flowers; harvest late September.
'**Tydeman's Early Worcester**' – Medium-sized, dark red eating and cooking apple with a rich, strawberry-like flavour. Partly self-fertile; early to mid-season flowers; harvest from August.
'**Winston**' – Eating apple with firm, juicy flesh. Disease-resistant. Partly self-fertile with late flowers; pick October onwards.
'**Worcester Pearmain**' – Aromatic, bright red eating apple with flavoursome, slightly lopsided fruit. Mid-season flowers; harvest from September.

Pollinating partners

Most types of fruit are self-fertile, but some apples, blueberries, pears and plums need to be fertilized by pollen from a different variety. On an allotment there are almost certain to be other fruit trees and bushes in the vicinity, but you might like to buy a 'pollinating partner', since you'll then have two types to enjoy. To ensure success, choose varieties with similar flowering seasons.

A rich-red eating apple with a strong, distinctive scent, 'Discovery' is crisp and flavoursome when fresh, but it doesn't keep well.

Blackberries

harvest JUL, AUG, SEP

Cultivated blackberry varieties, which are easy to grow, produce abundant, big, soft and sweetly juicy, mouth-blackening fruit, quite different from the small, often tart wild types. On allotments you'd be wise to choose a compact variety and consider a thornless one, too. You might also like to try one of the blackberry hybrids, such as loganberries and tayberries.

Cultivation

DIFFICULTY Very easy; little work needed apart from pruning.
PLANT One plant is usually enough (yield is about 4.5kg/10lb from a good modern variety, or 3.6kg/8lb from a very compact form). Blackberries are not too fussy and do well even in exposed areas, in shade and in heavy clay soils. Hybrid berries need more shelter and better soil.
SPACE Provide supports at least 1.2–1.5m (4–5ft) tall. Allow for a spread of 2m (6ft) for the most compact varieties, 2.5–4m (8–13ft) for larger modern varieties.
CARE Water well until established. Keep the ground well weeded; mulch heavily every spring with well-rotted organic matter, and in late April feed with a general-purpose fertilizer. Provide very good support. A fence or shed will do fine, but put up some wires to tie stems into. Alternatively, erect a post-and-wire support (*see* page 36). Thornless varieties can be trained over an arch. Use netting to protect fruit from birds.
HARVEST as soon as they are ripe – glossy, jet black and slightly soft to the touch, which could be from late summer, depending on the variety. Loganberries and tayberries tend to ripen earlier than most blackberries; like giant raspberries but with a tarter taste, their fruit turns a deep shade of purplish crimson when it is ripe and ready for picking.
STORAGE Blackberries are best eaten fresh but they freeze well, especially if already cooked. They also make good jelly or jam.

If you don't like thorns, choose one of the thornless blackberry varieties, such as 'Loch Ness', which also bears abundant fruit.

Pruning

NEW PLANTS In the first spring, or immediately after planting new canes, prune the strongest, thickest stems to within 25–30cm (10–12in) of soil level. Remove any thin, weak shoots. This will encourage the development of strong, vigorous shoots from the base. As the shoots grow, train them along wires. If any exceed 2m (6ft) long, remove the end 15cm (6in): this will encourage the formation of lateral, fruit-bearing shoots.
ESTABLISHED PLANTS Remove old stems that have already borne fruit to make room for new fruiting canes, and encourage the development of strong, vigorous shoots to replace those that will be removed after fruiting. The annual pruning takes place at the same time as training in a new set of canes (see page 42) and should be done very shortly after the fruit has been picked.

Look out for...

Raspberry beetles can spoil the fruit of loganberries and blackberries; otherwise, blackberries and their relatives are generally trouble-free. Just make sure you pick the fruit regularly before it spoils.

Worth trying...

BLACKBERRIES
'Fantasia' – Huge berries on vigorous, spiny canes; harvest from late August.
'Loch Ness' – Very compact with short, thornless canes that are almost self-supporting. Train like summer-fruiting raspberries (see pages 36 and 42). Conical berries from mid-August.
'Oregon Thornless' – Decorative leaves and spineless with comparatively well-behaved canes; harvest from late August.
'Veronique' – Ornamental variety with pink flowers, no thorns, and a compact, semi-upright habit – tie it to a post or fan it out over a fence panel. Produces good crops of large fruit in late summer.

HYBRID BERRIES
Some of these have named varieties with particular qualities, otherwise they are sold under their hybrid name.
'Black Butte' – Long, almost mulberry-like fruit on a fairly compact plant with stems to 2.5m (8ft); harvest from late July.
Boysenberry (blackberry hybrid) – Heavy crops of large, blackberry-like fruit with a great flavour in July and August. More drought-tolerant than true blackberries. Thornless varieties are widely available.
Loganberry (raspberry × dewberry) – Large, red, tangy fruit that is best cooked. The stems may reach 3m (10ft). **LY654** is thornless, with large berries from mid-July to early September. **LY59** has a good flavour but very thorny stems.
Tayberry (blackberry × raspberry) – Large, rich-red fruit, good raw or cooked. Generally considered to be the best of all the hybrid berries. May reach 3m (10ft). **'Buckingham'** is thornless with large, good-quality fruit in July and August.
Tummelberry (tayberry hybrid) – The tayberry-like fruit ripens in mid-July to late August. Much hardier than the tayberry and ideal for more exposed situations.

Blueberries are very attractive little shrubs, with pretty, white spring flowers, tasty berries and fiery autumn foliage.

Blueberries

harvest JUL, AUG, SEP

As well as tasting wonderful, blueberries are very good for you. They are a source of vitamin C and are full of antioxidants, which can give protection against many health problems. They require very acid conditions, so if you have alkaline soil, grow them in large pots or a raised bed filled with ericaceous (lime-free) compost. You need two varieties flowering at the same time for pollination (see box, page 83).

Cultivation

DIFFICULTY Moderate – giving them the right conditions is vital.
PLANT in sun or light dappled shade in rich, fertile, acid soil, ideally in spring.
SPACE 1.5m (5ft) apart.
CARE Add plenty of organic matter to the soil. The ground needs to be moist but to drain well, so work in grit. Also, use mycorrhizal fungal granules to improve your chances of success (see box, page 31). Water new plants regularly with soft water or rainwater, and keep them well watered in dry summers. No supports are needed. Each spring give a high-nitrogen

feed, and mulch very heavily with well-rotted organic matter; acidic types such as pine needles or bark chippings are best for blueberries. If plants are slow to make new growth, feed with 28g (1oz) of sulphate of ammonia per plant in late spring or early summer, and water in well.

HARVEST From midsummer to early autumn depending on the variety, pick individual berries as soon as they turn a deep, bloomy blue-black and feel soft.

STORAGE They will keep for up to two weeks in the fridge.

Pruning

After planting or in winter, remove dead or damaged shoots and cut back weak shoots by half to a healthy bud. Do this again the following winter. If you're strong-willed, remove flowers in the first two years to encourage the plant to grow more strongly. Thereafter, prune out one fifth to a quarter of the main stems to the base each year to encourage new wood. Select weak, horizontal or crossing shoots.

Look out for...

Blueberries have no real pest or disease problems in Britain, but they do need careful tending.

Worth trying...

'Bluecrop' – Large fruit on bushes 1.2m (4ft) high and 75cm (30in) across.
'Chandler' – Very large fruit on bushes 1.5m (5ft) tall.
'Earliblue' – Early fruit on bushes up to 2m (6ft) high and 90cm (3ft) wide.
'Spartan' – Large, pale blue fruit on bushes up to 2m (6ft) high.
'Sunshine Blue' – Heavy crops of flavoursome fruit on 90cm (3ft) plants.
'Top Hat' – Smallish fruit but with an excellent flavour on compact bushes 60cm (2ft) high.

Currants
(black, white and red)

harvest JUL, AUG

Well worth growing on an allotment, currants are versatile, tasty fruit that reward a little care with plentiful crops. They make great jams and jellies and are lovely in summer puddings. For a sweeter taste, and something a little different, try a jostaberry, which is a cross between a gooseberry and a blackcurrant.

Cultivation

DIFFICULTY Easy; little work.
PLANT in a sunny spot with rich, fertile soil that stays moist – blackcurrants enjoy boggy spots, while redcurrants can cope with some shade.
SPACE 1.5m (5ft) apart; most will reach about 1.2–1.5m (4–5ft) tall.

CARE Water well until established. Blackcurrants need a rich diet. Mulch generously every spring and feed with a general-purpose fertilizer. In early summer, give them an additional nitrogen-rich feed such as poultry manure pellets. Red and whitecurrants also like a spring mulch and a sprinkle of general-purpose fertilizer in mid-spring. Protect ripening fruit from birds.

HARVEST when they are very ripe and sweet. Leave them on the plants for as long as possible, but don't allow them to start dropping off. Pick the whole truss (or 'strig'). One way to separate the berries from the stalks is to hold the thick end of the stalk and pull the strig through the teeth of a dinner fork.

STORAGE They'll keep for a few days in the fridge, otherwise freeze, bottle or make jam.

Pruning

Blackcurrants and jostaberries are pruned slightly differently from redcurrants and whitecurrants. With blackcurrants and jostaberries, the first spring after planting, cut back all stems to a healthy bud, then prune annually in winter, removing one third of the oldest stems. Other currants are pruned like gooseberries. (For more on pruning currants, *see* page 41.)

Look out for…

Blister aphids attack the leaves, causing yellow blisters in blackcurrants and white-currants and red blistering on redcurrants. Check under the leaves for the aphids. In late June trim the affected stems almost back to the fruits; this will remove the affected leaves and serves as an interim trim, too. Gall midge maggots may distort and discolour young blackcurrant leaves. Pick off and destroy affected foliage. Blackcurrants may also suffer from big bud mites, which make the buds fat and rounded instead of long and slim. The same mites spread reversion disease, which reduces fruit crops. Check plants each spring and cut off stems with affected buds or grow resistant varieties. Sawflies can be a problem (see gooseberries, right). Orange-pink spots on dying shoots is a sign of coral spot. Prune off all affected stems.

Worth trying…

BLACKCURRANTS

'**Ben Connan**' – Very compact with large fruit from early to mid-July. Some pest and disease resistance.

'**Ben Hope**' – Large crops of medium-sized fruit in July. Pest- and disease-resistant, withstanding gall mites.

'**Ben Lomond**' – A heavy cropper producing large fruit at the end of July. Compact and rather upright, it needs very little pruning. '**Ben Nevis**' is similar but the bushes are bigger.

'**Ben Sarek**' – Plentiful crops of large berries from mid-July on dwarf bushes, to 90cm (3ft) high.

Jostaberry (blackcurrant × gooseberry) – Big, sweet fruit from early July and no gooseberry prickles. Fairly compact, it is resistant to blackcurrant pests and diseases. Once established, remove a third of the branches each winter.

RED AND WHITECURRANTS

'**Blanka**' – Very heavy-cropping white-currant ripening in late July and August.

'**Jonkheer van Tets**' – Redcurrant with long trusses of large berries in early July.

'**Red Lake**' – Redcurrant with large crops of juicy berries carried on long trusses in early July.

'**Stanza**' – Small, dark red currants in late July and August. The flowers open late, so are not affected by late frosts.

'**White Versailles**' – Whitecurrant with large, sweet fruit ripening in July.

Gooseberries

harvest MAY, JUN, JUL

Gooseberries are prickly little shrubs with hairy green, yellow or pinkish fruit that is great for desserts and jams as well as for eating fresh. Dessert gooseberries are relative newcomers, but they're very welcome and delicious, cooked or raw. If you are going to grow only one gooseberry, make it a dessert variety.

Cultivation

DIFFICULTY Easy; moderate input.
PLANT in a sunny, sheltered place in well-drained, fertile soil.
SPACE 90cm (3ft) apart.
CARE Each spring, add a generous mulch underneath the plants, and in mid- to late April sprinkle on a general-purpose fertilizer. Water in dry spells in summer. Thin the fruit in stages between late May

As well as being a lovely red colour, gooseberry 'Pax' has a sweet and tasty flavour.

and June. You can cook the removed fruit. Leave half the original crop evenly spaced over the bush to fill out and ripen. Use netting or grow in a fruit cage to protect fruit against birds.

HARVEST Pick the green cooking varieties as soon as they are big enough, often as early as May. The smaller the fruit, the more sour they taste, so you'll need more sugar when cooking. Dessert gooseberries are not completely ripe until July.

STORAGE Cook and use in pies or jams. They can be frozen raw.

Pruning

Cut all the stems of gooseberry bushes back by half after planting. Do other pruning from November to February, with a little tidying in summer (see page 41).

Look out for…

American gooseberry mildew forms a white, powdery 'bloom' over the tips of young shoots, leaves and fruit. Wipe this off the fruit and prune out the affected shoot-tips after the fruit has been picked. Prevent mildew by pruning to improve air circulation around the plants, and feed with 28g (1oz) of sulphate of potash per plant in spring instead of general-purpose fertilizer. Grow resistant varieties.

The 'looper' caterpillars of the magpie moth (white, with black and orange markings) can strip the bushes of leaves in May and June. Remove them by hand.

Dull khaki caterpillars, on the leaf undersides from early May to late summer, are the larvae of the gooseberry sawfly. A bad infestation can quickly defoliate the bushes. Again, remove them by hand.

Worth trying…

'**Greenfinch**' – Smooth green fruit that ripens in July; compact, mildew-resistant.

'**Hinomaki Red**' – Large, sweet dessert fruit that ripens to red in July. Mildew-resistant. '**Hinomaki Yellow**' ripens to pale gold.

'**Invicta**' – A traditional thorny variety with heavy crops of tasty, tangy green fruit in June. Mildew-resistant.

'**Pax**' – Heavy cropping, thornless, red dessert gooseberry with fruit that ripens from late June to July. Mildew-resistant.
'**Whinham's Industry**' – Similar to 'Pax', but thorny, with fruit in July; succeeds in shade and heavy soil.

Grapes

harvest AUG, SEP, OCT

On an allotment the best way to grow grapes is using posts and wires, as this enables you to obtain the most fruit possible in a small area. You need to prune regularly and be prepared to remove a proportion of flowers and young grapes. In most years, this will ensure a reasonable harvest of well-flavoured fruit. If you have a greenhouse or polytunnel you are more assured of a good crop, but the varieties listed here are reliable outdoor performers.

Cultivation

DIFFICULTY Quite demanding.
PLANT in a warm, sunny, sheltered spot, in well-drained, fertile soil with lots of well-rotted organic matter. Provide a good support system of posts and wires.
SPACE 1.5m (5ft) apart in rows 2–2.5m (6–8ft) apart.
CARE Mulch generously each spring and sprinkle a handful of general fertilizer and 15g (½oz) of sulphate of potash over the soil around the base of each vine in April. Keep vines well watered in dry spells in the summer while they are carrying fruit.
HARVEST when they are completely ripe. Depending on the variety, grapes can be ready from late August to the end of October. Cut the whole bunch.
STORAGE They will keep for up to two weeks in the fridge and can be frozen whole and used to make smoothies.

Pruning

Grapes need careful pruning to produce good crops. The easiest way is called the rod-and-spur method (*see* page 42), where

the stems are trained along horizontal wires and kept tightly pruned to prevent too much leafy growth. It is also important to restrict the number of grape bunches to a maximum of one every 30cm (12in), so that the vine puts energy into producing a few large, juicy grapes rather than many small ones.

Look out for...

Birds will happily eat all of an outdoor crop, so protect bunches with small nets or whole plants with a sheet of netting.

Worth trying...

'**Boskoop Glory**' – A reliable black grape for both wine-making and eating.
'**Brandt**' – A dual-purpose, ornamental and dessert grape with small bunches of small, sweet, black grapes. It also has great autumn foliage colour. Crops without undue attention.
'**Dornfelder**' – Large, sweet, dark red grapes in good-sized bunches in autumn.
'**Müller Thurgau**' – The classic home-grown wine vine, but also good for eating in dry summers when planted in a warm, sunny spot.

'Boskoop Glory' is an all-round performer that makes good wine but is also a pleasant dessert grape.

'**Perlette**' – Thin-skinned, sweet and seedless green grapes that ripen early.
'**Strawberry**' – Bunches of copper-pink to amber fruit that ripens late in the season.

Kiwi fruit

harvest OCT

Kiwis are delicious, juicy and tangy and are well worth trying on the allotment, especially now that self-fertile outdoor varieties are available. Before this you had to grow at least two plants indoors – and they may be attractive but they are also big, with a tendency to take over when your back's turned.

Cultivation

DIFFICULTY Moderate.
PLANT in a warm, sunny, sheltered spot with humus-rich, fertile, well-drained soil.
SPACE Allow 3–4.5m (10–15ft) all around each plant.
CARE Provide a strong framework of trellis or wires and train the plants well. Tie in

If pruned regularly, the kiwi 'Bruno' can produce reasonable crops of large, elongated fruits, especially in a warm summer.

new growth regularly in summer. Mulch generously in spring, and sprinkle a handful of general-purpose fertilizer and 15g (½oz) of sulphate of potash over the soil under each plant in April.

HARVEST in October, or later if it has been a poor summer. When ready, they will be softly firm and will taste sweet. If an early frost or severe weather is forecast, drape fleece over the plants.

STORAGE Arrange in a single layer in trays in a cool room, garage or shed, where they should keep for up to six weeks.

Pruning

Kiwi plants are best trained on horizontal wires about 30–50cm (12–20in) apart. The aim is to create a number of tiers of horizontal stems (laterals) that will carry fruiting spurs.

Allow the stems to harden before tying them in. Don't allow them to twine around the support. If you need to restrict the vine's spread, prune in late winter or early spring; laterals need replacing after a few years, so prune them back to a bud near their base and train the resulting new growth.

To prune for greater fruit production, follow the rod-and-spur method in summer (*see* page 42).

If you don't have room for many kiwi fruit plants, have one of each sex and plant both in the same hole. Train them in the same way, but have one upright stem for each plant and train alternate male and female stems out along your wires.

Look out for…

Cultivation problems may occur, such as small fruit that doesn't ripen. This is usually due to cold weather or too little sun. In an exposed or northerly situation, it's best to grow kiwis in a greenhouse or a polytunnel.

Worth trying…

'Abbott' and **'Bruno'** – Both have good crops; fruit of 'Bruno' is slightly larger; both need pollinating partners.
'Jenny' – Self-fertile with small, very sweet fruit. Not very hardy.
'Hayward' – Not over-vigorous and flowers quite late; 'Tomuri' is a good pollinating partner.

Siberian kiwi

The Siberian kiwi or Mongolian gooseberry (*Actinidia arguta* 'Issai') is more compact than conventional kiwis and has small, sweet, smooth-skinned, gooseberry-sized fruit that ripens more reliably and slightly earlier. It's ideal for colder or smaller gardens. Grow the plant as a single slanting or horizontal stem tied to a supporting pole or on a wire across a fence or shed; prune the laterals to 20cm (8in) long each winter to form branching fruiting spurs.

Melons

If you have ever tasted sweetly juicy melons fresh from the vine, you'll want to try growing them yourself. Canteloupes are the best choice. However, melons are not easy. They need a long, hot summer and careful attention.

Sow seed in small pots indoors in mid-spring. Pot the seedlings up into gradually larger pots, taking care not to damage the stems. Plant them in a sunny, sheltered spot in humus-rich, warm soil in early summer, protecting them with a cloche or cold frame at first. If you have a polytunnel or greenhouse, all the better.

Grow the vines horizontally, but keep them off the ground using landscaping fabric or netting stretched tight and supported on bricks.

Water carefully – too much water causes rotting. Feed weekly once the first flower has opened. Trim the sideshoots to two leaves beyond the developing fruit and limit the number of fruit per vine to two or three. Protect the plants with fleece during cool weather.

Pears

harvest AUG, SEP, OCT

Unlike their close relations the apples, pears can be tricky to grow – they're quite fussy about growing conditions and are relatively slow to come to fruit. On the plus side, they suffer fewer pests and diseases than apples. On an allotment, you're most likely to grow pears as cordons against a sunny fence or shed wall (*see* page 40) – you'll need at least two varieties that are suitable pollinating partners for reliable cropping (*see* box, page 83). If you have the space for a freestanding tree, and your allotment rules permit you to grow one, make sure that you plant a family pear, which consists of branches of several different varieties grafted onto a single trunk; the benefit of this is that you need only one tree because the varieties are pollinating partners (an added bonus is you get several different types of pear on one tree).

Cultivation

DIFFICULTY Challenging; moderate to high input.
PLANT in a warm, sunny, sheltered spot with fertile, well-drained soil. If you haven't selected a family pear tree, provide a suitable pollinating partner for your pear. Even self-fertile varieties crop far better when cross-pollinated. 'Conference' or 'Concorde' are safe bets, even if you don't know the name of your own variety.
SPACE Plant cordons 75cm (30in) apart.
CARE Keep newly planted trees watered in dry spells for their first summer. Each spring, mulch generously and from mid- to late April feed with general-purpose fertilizer.

In a dry summer, water trees while they are carrying a crop of fruit, especially those against a wall or fence, which suffer more from drought.
HARVEST From late August onwards; some late varieties hang on until mid-October.

When to pick pears

Visually, there is little warning; there is only a minor colour change, the skin turning very slightly lighter, and some varieties may develop a faint, warm flush, but you might get a hint by the first windfalls. Test your hunch by lifting a pear in a cupped hand; if it lifts off the tree complete with its stalk, it's ready, otherwise leave it slightly longer.

Harvesting is tricky: you need to pick the pears at exactly the right moment and bring them in to finish them off, and it's not easy to recognize this moment (*see* box, above). Don't leave them on the trees to ripen fully, as this makes them go 'sleepy' (brown or mealy-textured inside). Check them constantly, especially if bad weather is forecast, otherwise they may be knocked off the trees and spoiled.

STORAGE Pears need to be stored before they are ready to eat. Keep them under cover in a cool place, such as a shed or garage; bring them in a few at a time as they reach their peak time – they'll ripen within a few days.

Don't bring pears straight indoors from the garden: late pears in particular will either stay rock hard or turn 'sleepy'.

Pruning

Prune freestanding pear trees lightly in winter, removing damaged, diseased and dead wood, and prune cordons in late July (*see* page 40).

Look out for…

Like apples, pears can be affected by fireblight and scab. The latter is a fungal disease that causes black or brown cracks with corky edges on the fruit, which can be misshapen, and khaki blotches on the leaves, plus premature leaf fall. (*See also* Apples, pages 82–3.)

Pear leaf blister mite can affect pears in dry conditions, such as growing against fences or walls. The leaves develop yellow or red blisters that eventually turn black. Pick off and burn leaves as soon as you spot a problem.

One of the most reliable pears, 'Conference' has juicy flesh that is delicious fresh or cooked. It is also a good pollinator for other pears.

Pear midges are grubs that roll up the leaves. Pick off and burn affected leaves.

Small, stunted fruit is a result of either poor growing conditions or poor pollination. Feed and mulch the tree very well each spring, cover it with fleece on cold nights around flowering time, and plant a pollinator. Above all, guard against poor, dry soil. On chalky soil pears can sometimes suffer from iron deficiency, so feed with sequestered iron.

Worth trying…

'**Beurré Superfin**' – Yellow, slightly russeted skin and sweet, juicy flesh. Pick September; ready October – the fruit does not keep for long. 'Conference' is a suitable pollinator.

'**Concorde**' ('Conference' × 'Doyenné du Comice') – Reliable and easy with light green fruit with faint brown russeting. Pick September; use October and November. Self-fertile; a good pollinator of many varieties.

'**Conference**' – Elongated, greeny-brown fruit, for eating and cooking; very reliable and heavy cropping. Pick September; use October and November. Not self-fertile, as is often suggested, but usually manages to crop well even if it is the only pear in the immediate locality. It is a good pollinator for many varieties.

'**Doyenné du Comice**' – A large, fat dessert pear with pale green skin that is heavily covered with brown russeting and faint red 'cheeks'. It has very rich, juicy, melting flesh. Pick mid-October; use November and December. 'Conference' is a good pollinator.

'**Onward**' – Similar to 'Doyenné du Comice', but ready earlier. Pick in mid-September; use in late September. Does not keep. 'Concorde' is a suitable pollinating partner.

'**Red Williams**' – Similar to 'Doyenné du Comice' but with red-skinned fruit when ripe. Pick from late August; use throughout September. Cross-pollinated by 'Conference'.

Plums, damsons and greengages

harvest JUL, AUG, SEP, OCT

Plums are mostly grown as freestanding trees, but cordons are occasionally available and are useful as they take up less space. Although many plums are not self-fertile, there is often another plum in the area, so pollinating partners (*see* box, page 83) are not always needed. The plum family includes lovely old-fashioned fruit such as damsons, greengages, mirabelles and those hedgerow-dwellers sloes and bullaces. Many were favourites in cottage gardens.

Cultivation

DIFFICULTY Easy; low input (cordons are more demanding).

PLANT in a sheltered, sunny spot in fertile, well-drained soil.

SPACE Plant cordons 90cm (3ft) apart.

CARE Keep new plants watered in dry spells for their first summer. Mulch generously each spring and in April

Damsons are an attractive rich-purple fruit with a soft white bloom on the skin. They can be used to make jam and jelly.

sprinkle a double handful of general-purpose fertilizer over the soil beneath each tree. As fruits begin ripening, protect them with netting to keep birds off.

Thin out a heavy crop once it has set – the plums will be green and half-size. 'Victoria' in particular is renowned for cropping very heavily every other year and taking a year off in between to recover, and crop-thinning helps to prevent this. It also avoids the branches snapping under the weight of the fruit. Snip fruit off at the stalk with secateurs, leaving the biggest and best 5–8cm (2–3in) apart along the branches.

HARVEST in summer and autumn, as soon as the first few ripe windfalls begin to drop. Choose well-coloured fruits that are soft and drop into your hands with a gentle pull. Leave plum stalks on the branch and keep the stalk on the fruit for damsons and greengages. Depending on the variety, you could be picking plums and greengages from late July to the end of September and damsons in September and October.

Victoria plums are soft, sweet, juicy fruit that are ideal eaten straight from the tree, but are also good in pies, crumbles and jam.

STORAGE Make jams and jellies or pies. You can also freeze plums, but remove the stones first.

Pruning

Generally it is best to avoid pruning plums and damsons because it may encourage silver leaf disease. However, if you are training cordons or need to restrict growth or remove damaged branches, prune in late spring or summer, when the trees are growing strongly and are most able to resist diseases.

Look out for...

Little or no fruit may be due to a lack of a suitable pollinator (even so-called

self-fertile varieties produce bigger and better crops if there's a pollinator near by), or biennial bearing caused by allowing a heavy cropper to carry enormous crops without thinning.

If the leaves take on a silvery sheen, turn brown and die, your plum has silver leaf disease.

Gummy lumps appearing on otherwise healthy bark may be caused by stress or poor cultivation techniques.

Worth trying...

'Czar' – Heavy crops of medium-sized, oval, purple fruit. Used for cooking. Self-fertile. Ripens in early August.

'Marjorie's Seedling' – One of the very best cooking plums, but also good for eating, with large, oval, purple-skinned fruit. Self-fertile. Ripens in late September and early October.

'Merryweather' – A self-fertile damson with large, round, purple fruit. Ripens in September.

Myrobalan or **cherry plum** (*Prunus cerasifera*) – Very small, round plums that look like cherries. Self-fertile, and ripens in late July. There are also named hybrids that produce red or yellow fruit. They cross-pollinate each other, but they are also pollinated by 'Victoria'.

'Old Green Gage' – Small, flavoursome, yellowy-green gages, but with rather light and irregular crops; ripens late August/early September. Pollinated by 'Marjorie's Seedling'.

'Ouillin's Golden Gage' – Heavy crops of tasty dessert fruits ripening in early August from pale green to red-streaked gold. A gage-like plum that could almost be mistaken for an apricot. Pollinated by 'Victoria'.

'Victoria' – This heavy-cropping favourite is a dessert plum but it is also used for cooking. It has large, oval, very sweet, juicy fruit: rich red, flushed pale gold and darker red. The plums ripen from the end of August into September, slightly earlier in a hot summer. If you can grow only one variety, it is likely to be 'Victoria' – the perfect dual-purpose, self-fertile plum tree.

Raspberries

harvest JUN, JUL, AUG, SEP, OCT, NOV

If you are new to fruit-growing and are wondering where to begin, raspberries are a very good choice: they are perfect eaten as they are or in summery puddings and also make good, if pippy, jam. Shop-bought raspberries are often tasteless and a bit solid in texture (or squishy and overripe) and they're also expensive. If you grow a selection of your own, you can pick them when they're ripe and enjoy them through summer and into autumn, for next to nothing. They also freeze very well, too.

Cultivation

DIFFICULTY Easy; moderate input.
PLANT in good, fertile, well-drained, neutral or slightly acid soil full of organic matter. The canes need a sheltered spot that gets the sun for half the day at least.
SPACE plants 45cm (18in) apart. Rows should be 2m (6ft) apart for summer-fruiting varieties, 90cm (3ft) for autumn varieties. Provide adequate support up to about 2m (6ft) high (*see* page 36).
CARE In spring, sprinkle general-purpose fertilizer along each side of the row and mulch the plants heavily with well-rotted organic matter. Water during dry spells through summer and into autumn – if they don't get enough water when cropping you'll get fewer small, hard fruit. It's best not to allow autumn-fruiting raspberries to fruit in the first year as this enables them to establish better.
HARVEST when they are fully ripe by leaving them on the canes until a day or two after they have turned red (or yellow). Give the fruit a gentle pull between thumb and forefinger; if it doesn't come away, leaving the plug on the plant, it isn't ready. The fruit ripens from late June into August, and as late as November in a good year (frosts put paid to the fruit).
STORAGE Raspberries are best eaten fresh, but small, slightly underripe berries can be frozen.

Pruning

After planting, remove any thin, weak or distorted shoots and loosely tie the rest to the support. As the canes grow, tie them to the support wires. If the canes grow much taller than the top wire, cut them off 15cm (6in) above it.

Summer-fruiting raspberries fruit on canes produced the previous year, so the idea behind pruning is to remove these after they have fruited (they won't fruit again) and to encourage a healthy number of new canes that will then supply next year's fruits.

Autumn-fruiting raspberries bear the best crop on canes produced in the current year, so you prune to encourage them to produce plenty of these. In late winter or before bud burst, cut all the canes to 8cm (3in) above the ground. In early summer thin the canes to 8–10cm (3–4in) apart, removing any less than 1m (40in) high. Tie in the remaining canes.

(For more on pruning raspberries, *see* page 42.)

Look out for...

Birds love raspberries, so cover rows with netting as soon as the first few berries start turning pink.

Several viruses affect raspberries, stunting the plants and reducing the yield; they also cause yellow blotches or mottling on the foliage. There is no cure, just dig up and destroy affected canes. Replace old plants after ten years in any case, as they will have much reduced in vigour by then. Plant the next lot in a new patch of ground.

Yellowing leaves, stunted growth and poor yield usually point to lime-induced chlorosis (a result of an over-alkaline soil). If growing raspberries in even slightly alkaline soil, apply sulphur powder or sulphur chips to the ground in spring, or use a chelated iron feed (sequestrene) of the sort used for rhododendrons and camellias. Repeat this treatment each year, in early spring.

Cane blight and cane spot are two serious diseases producing black-based or

'Autumn Bliss' is a good late-fruiting choice and needs little in the way of attention.

purple-spotted canes. There is no cure, although fungicides may keep cane spot under control. It is better to destroy affected canes, plant new specimens in fresh ground, or grow a resistant variety.

Fruit that is dry and brown at the stalk end may contain the larvae of raspberry beetles. There is no treatment, but if you spot the egg-laying adults, which are 4mm (less than ¼in) long and brown, it is best to squash them immediately.

Worth trying...

'All Gold' – Autumn-fruiting with well-flavoured, yellow fruit from end of July.
'Autumn Bliss' – Autumn-fruiting with tasty, medium-sized, red fruit from mid-August. Does not need supporting.
'Glen Ample' – Summer-fruiting ripening from late June. Spine-free.
'Leo' – Summer-fruiting with tangy, red fruit from late July. Disease-resistant.
'Malling Admiral' – Summer-fruiting ripening from mid-July. Good disease resistance and spineless.
'Malling Jewel' – Summer-fruiting ripening in early July; excellent flavour. Good resistance to virus.

Rhubarb

harvest MAR, APR, MAY, JUN, JUL

Rhubarb should have a place in everyone's allotment. It is tasty and versatile, making the best pies and crumbles you're ever likely to eat, and it's good for you, too. Its only drawback is that you usually do need to use sugar on it. Forced rhubarb (*see* box, below) is a delicacy, since forcing makes the stems grow earlier, more slender and very succulent.

Cultivation

DIFFICULTY Easy; low input.

PLANT in very heavily manured, reasonably heavy soil; if you can, put it near the compost heap where it will enjoy the rich runoff in the soil. Give it full sun so the stems will develop a redder colour and a sweeter, richer flavour. To create new plants, divide the rootball and replant the pieces.

SPACE Allow at least 90cm (3ft) around each plant.

CARE Water well. Remove flowering stems in summer. Cut them out as close to the base as you can without harming the plant. Every autumn as the foliage dies down, remove the dead leaves, sprinkle general-purpose fertilizer around the plants and mulch with organic matter.

HARVEST between March and July, but then allow the plant to grow naturally for the rest of the season so it recovers. Pick

'Timperley Early' is one of the best rhubarbs for forcing, but it can also be eaten later in the season.

well-coloured stems whose leaves have just opened out fully: these are the most tasty and tender. Don't cut the stems: hold the stalk near the base and tug and twist so it comes out cleanly, including the bit that clasps round the top of the root. Trim this and remove the leaves before cooking.

STORAGE Rhubarb must be cooked before eating and can be frozen raw or cooked.

Look out for...

Dull, listless foliage, small, sickly stems and the growth buds dying off are symptoms of crown rot. There is no cure; remove and destroy affected plants and plant new ones in a different spot.

Worth trying...

'Hawke's Champagne' (or 'Champagne') – Excellent flavour with thick, heavily red-flushed green stems. Harvest in spring and early summer.

'Stockbridge Arrow' – Very tasty with thick, rich pink-red stems. This is a very early variety that is bred especially for

forcing in heat but it can also be cultivated in the conventional way.

'Timperley Early' – A very early variety; when forced, it will crop from February onwards; you can often pick a few slender stems as late as July or August too.

Strawberries

harvest JUN, JUL, AUG, SEP, OCT

Once you've tasted home-grown strawberries, you'll never want to eat any other kind. They smell lovely, they're brightly coloured, soft, juicy and full of flavour. Another benefit is that you can grow a selection of varieties that ripen at different times, taste different and have fruit of varying sizes. Each plant yields roughly 225g (8oz) of fruit, so plant enough for your needs. You can easily get more plants by potting up plantlets produced on the runners, which grow throughout the summer. In fact, they often root by themselves.

Cultivation

DIFFICULTY Reasonably easy.

PLANT Ideally, put in young plants in August or September so they're well established for cropping the following summer; alternatively, plant in late autumn or early spring and put up with a smaller first-year crop. Choose a sunny, sheltered spot with humus-rich, fertile, well-drained soil. Avoid planting strawberries where you've grown potatoes, tomatoes or chrysanthemums; all these plants are prone to verticillium wilt, which can kill the fruit. Strawberries also grow very well in containers.

SPACE Where possible, space each plant 45cm (18in) apart in rows 90cm (3ft) apart. In a raised bed with deep, rich soil you can grow them 30–38cm (12–15in) apart with 60cm (2ft) between rows.

CARE In early spring apply 15g (½oz) of sulphate of potash per square metre (square yard) of strawberry bed, sprinkling it carefully between the plants.

Forcing rhubarb

Any well-established rhubarb can be encouraged to produce some very early, thin, blanched stems, as shown above. Cover the crown with a rhubarb-forcing pot, or an upturned dustbin or similar large container in mid-January or early February. Ideally, put straw around the pot for insulation. Within a few weeks, long stems with pale yellowy-coloured leaves appear. Pull as many of these as you want until the end of March, but then uncover the plant and allow it to grow naturally, taking only a small crop of stems for the rest of that season.

In early summer, as the first small, green fruits appear, spread straw or lay synthetic strawberry mats between the plants (*see* page 38). Tuck these under the foliage and around the 'collar' of the plants to smother weeds and protect the fruit from splashes, which can make it turn mouldy. Water carefully between the plants.

Protect the plants from birds with netting. After the whole crop has been picked, clip strawberry plants over with a pair of shears to remove all the old fruit stems, leaves and runners, and finally feed the bed with a general-purpose fertilizer and water it in well. The plants soon make healthy, fresh new growth that sets them up for cropping well again next year. Strawberry plants crop well for three or four years, after which they are best replaced with new plants.

HARVEST when perfectly ripe. Once the strawberries have turned red, give them a couple more days to fatten up and really ripen. Pick over plants daily, and don't leave small or misshapen ones behind, as they'll go mouldy and may spread disease. Use them in cooking or jam instead.

STORAGE Strawberries should be eaten straight from the garden, but a glut will make good jam.

Look out for…

Slugs and snails are the bane of the strawberry grower. Keep weeds down and clear any debris under which they might hide. In raised beds with wooden edges, consider using copper strips. You tack the strip along the edge of the bed and this gives the slugs a mild electric shock, which deters them from venturing further.

Grey mould, or botrytis, can affect strawberries. It is worse in damp summers or if the fruit is splashed when you're watering. Keep weeds controlled and space plants fairly well apart to improve air circulation; avoid spraying with fungicide, particularly if you want to use the fruit in preserves. (It's usually too late by the time fruit is going mouldy anyway.)

Yellow, blotchy leaves and progressively low yields are due to strawberry virus,

Alpine strawberries

These are dwarf plants producing tiny fruit that is sweet and bursting with flavour. The plants are grown from seed, as they don't produce runners. Sow in early spring under glass or on a bright windowsill indoors, and prick out the seedlings into 8cm (3in) pots when large enough to handle. Plant out the young plants 23cm (9in) apart in summer. You might get some fruit the same summer.

particularly if the plants are several years old or you propagate your own plants from runners. The virus is spread by greenfly, so you'll usually get it eventually. Dig out and destroy affected plants as soon as you see the problem, before it can be spread to the others, and buy virus-free stock to start a new row at the first opportunity. Zap greenfly to prevent them spreading the disease in the first place.

Verticillium wilt is often fatal. It makes the leaves wilt then turn brown. There is no cure, so remove affected plants, and surrounding soil if possible, as soon as you spot a problem.

Red core is a disease of heavy or damp soils. It stunts the plants, which grow reddish leaves and may collapse. If red core strikes, destroy your current plants, change the site and improve drainage.

Worth trying…

'**Cambridge Favourite**' – Medium-sized, tasty fruit from late June to late July; produces heavy crops on easily grown, disease-resistant plants.

'**Cambridge Late Pine**' – Wonderful flavour from dark red, beautifully fragrant fruit; ripens mid-June to mid-July.

'**Elsanta**' – Large crops of well-flavoured berries; mid-June to mid-July. Highly reliable – a good beginner's variety.

'**Flamenco**' – A so-called 'perpetual fruiter', with heavy crops of deliciously flavoured fruit in flushes from late August until autumn frosts.

'**Florence**' – Late cropper with large, firm fruit ripening from early July to early August. Good disease resistance.

'**Honeoye**' – Flavoursome fruit throughout June. Some grey mould resistance.

'**Mae**' – Grown for its early fruiting abilities – mid- to late May if protected with cloches in spring, otherwise ready in June and early July.

'**Mara des Bois**' – A 'perpetual fruiter' with a lovely flavour of wild strawberries; fruits from late summer into autumn.

'**Pegasus**' – Sweet-flavoured, medium to large strawberries towards the end of June. Disease-resistant.

'**Royal Sovereign**' – An old favourite that can't quite compete with modern varieties, but has an outstanding flavour. Light crops of small fruit in early June to mid-July. Be prepared to pamper it.

'Florence' is a widely available and reliable, late cropper producing large, juicy fruit.

Index

Page numbers in *italics* refer to plants featured in the A–Z of vegetables, herbs and fruit.

Acknowledgements

BBC Books and OutHouse would like to thank the following for their assistance in preparing this book: Robin Whitecross for picture research; Lesley Riley for proofreading; Marie Lorimer for the index.

Picture credits

Key t = top, b = bottom, l = left, r = right, c = centre

PHOTOGRAPHS

All photographs by Jonathan Buckley except those listed below.

GAP Photos Lee Avison 32(3); Mark Bolton 10, 15(1), 23; Elke Borkowski 58, 87t; Nicola Browne 9, 19; FhF Greenmedia 53b; Suzie Gibbons 11; John Glover 43(2), 51b, 79t, 85b, 86; Michael Howes 30t; Martin Hughes-Jones 62b; Janet Johnson 5r, 87t; Lynn Keddie 2/3; Geoff Kidd 43(1); Michael King 12t, 36; Fiona Lea 14, 46; Howard Rice 32(1), 61, 91; JS Sira 67r; Friedrich Strauss 88; Maddie Thornhill 13; Mark Winwood 12b

Garden Collection Jane Sebire 67l

Garden Picture Library/Getty Images Ron Evans 16; Howard Rice 77b

Garden World Images Martin Hughes-Jones 76t; John Martin 60b

Sue Gordon 17t, 27(3), 31tl & tr, 37, 38t, 44

Andrew McIndoe 27(2), 32(2), 54, 55t, 63, 73t & b, 75b, 78

Robin Whitecross 4, 5l, 8, 15(3), 25, 27(1), 35b, 43(3), (4) & (5), 51t, 52, 55b, 57t, 59, 60t, 69b, 71t & b, 81(4), 84b

ILLUSTRATIONS

Lizzie Harper 22, 28bl & br, 30, 34, 36, 39t, bl & br, 40, 41, 42, 44b, 45d, 47a, d & g

Sue Hillier 44a, 45a, b, c, e & f, 46a, b, c, d, e , 47b, c, e & f

Thanks are also due to the gardeners whose plots (including those listed below) appear in the book:

Castle Allotments, Arundel 13; Ashton Vale Allotments, Bristol 15(1), 23; Fulham Palace Meadows Allotments, London 9; Park Road Allotments, Winchester 17t, 31tr, 37; Rofford Manor, Oxfordshire 31; Swanage Town Allotments 25; Walsham-le-Willows Allotments, Suffolk 12t

While every effort has been made to trace and acknowledge all copyright holders, the publisher would like to apologize should there be any errors or omissions.